Lion House Christmas

SHADOW
MOUNTAIN

Design and photo art direction by Shauna Gibby. Photography by John Luke. Food styling by Maxine Bramwell. Cover lettering by James Fedor and John Gibby.

© 2006 Temple Square Hospitality Corporation

Visit us at shadowmountain.com

Library of Congress Cataloging-in-Publication Data

Lion house Christmas. — Rev. ed.
    p. cm.
  Includes index.
  ISBN-10 1-59038-615-9 (hardbound : alk. paper)
  ISBN-13 978-1-59038-615-6 (hardbound : alk. paper)
  1. Christmas cookery.
  TX739.2.C45L56 2006
  641.5'686—dc22   2006012411

Printed in China
R. R. Donnelley and Sons, Schenzhen, China

10   9   8   7   6   5   4   3   2   1

Contents

Lion House Parlor

Preface

From the time it was built in 1856, The Lion House has been a place for joyous Christmas gatherings. The Victorian-era decorations and the delectable aromas of home-cooked food remind present-day guests of holiday festivities from the past.

Lion House Christmas is a collection of traditional and modern recipes selected to help you prepare delicious meals and create cherished memories.

Invite your friends to share the warmth of homemade soup and freshly baked bread. Host a family dinner of succulent roast turkey with all the trimmings. Share a festive gift of holiday treats with your neighbors.

Whatever your plans are for celebrating the season, this book will become a treasured resource.

Acknowledgments

We are grateful to all the Lion House employees who spent countless hours reviewing, revising, testing, and adding recipes: Brenda Hopkin, Julie Ulrich, Barbara Carling, David Bench, Ann Sudweeks, Alba Arceo, Patrick Roe, Leonel Perez, Lesieli Tulikifanga, Leticia Lezama, Ive Thomas, Paula Moscoso, Rebekah Jones, Shauna Williams, Neal Allen, Rafael Mauricio, Howard Johnson, Joseph Norberg, Abram Farr, Marshal Underwood, and Ivoni McPhie. Many recipes are from the original Lion House Christmas cookbook. Without the special care and pride shown by all who work at the Lion House, this book would not have been possible.

Thanks also to the many people at Deseret Book: Jana Erickson, Janna DeVore, Lisa Mangum, Shauna Gibby, Tonya Facemyer, and Laurie Cook.

We also express thanks to Shauna Gibby for her design and art direction, Maxine Bramwell for her expertise in food styling, and John Luke for the beautiful photography.

Special thanks to the following businesses and individuals for loaning us dishes and linens for the photos: Meier & Frank, Mervyn's, Target, Debbie Brady, Maxine Bramwell, Jana Erickson, Shauna Gibby, Brenda Hopkin, Dianna Hymas, and Julie Ulrich.

St. Nick's Lime Fizz and Chicken Puffs

Refreshing Beverages and Appetizers

St. Nick's Lime Fizz

5 fresh limes, juiced (about ½ cup)
½ cup sugar
1½ cups pineapple juice
1 quart lime sherbet
1 16-ounce bottle lemon-lime soda
   Maraschino cherries, for
      garnishing
8 thin half-slices lime, for garnishing

Place lime juice, sugar, and pineapple juice in a blender and process for 30 seconds. Add half of the lime sherbet and process again for a few seconds. Pour juice mixture into eight 10-ounce glasses (two-thirds full). Fill glasses almost to the top with lemon-lime soda. Top each cup with a scoop of sherbet. Garnish with a maraschino cherry and a half-slice of fresh lime. Serve with straws. Makes 8 servings.

Spiced Cranberry Cocktail

4 cups (1 32-ounce bottle) cranberry
      juice cocktail
2 cups orange juice
1 cup unsweetened grapefruit juice
½ cup grenadine syrup
¼ teaspoon ground cloves
¼ teaspoon ground nutmeg

Combine ingredients in a large saucepan and heat over medium heat until warm. Makes 15 half-cup servings.

LION HOUSE WASSAIL

2¼ cups sugar
4 cups water
2 cinnamon sticks
8 allspice berries
10 whole cloves
1 piece fresh ginger
4 cups orange juice
2 cups lemon juice
2 quarts apple cider or juice

Combine sugar and water in a large pot; boil 5 minutes. Remove pot from heat and add cinnamon sticks, allspice berries, cloves, and ginger. Cover and let stand in a warm place for 1 hour; strain. Just before serving, add juices and cider and bring quickly to boil. Remove from heat and serve. Makes 36 half-cup servings.

WARM ORANGE-ALMOND DRINK

3 cups sugar
4 cups water
1 12-ounce can frozen orange
   juice concentrate
1½ cups lemon juice
1 tablespoon almond extract
2 teaspoons vanilla
¼ teaspoon each ground cloves,
   allspice, and cinnamon
   (optional)
4 quarts water

Heat sugar and 4 cups water in a large pot over medium heat. Stir in remaining ingredients and heat until hot but not boiling. Serve warm. Leftover beverage can be cooled and stored in the refrigerator for ten days. Makes 48 half-cup servings.

HOLIDAY NOG

¼ cup sugar
½ teaspoon ground cinnamon
¼ teaspoon ground ginger
1½ cups liquid pasteurized eggs
   (6 whole eggs can be used at
   your own discretion)
4 cups orange juice
4 cups pineapple juice
4 cups ginger ale
1 pint orange sherbet

In a large bowl, combine sugar, cinnamon, and ginger. Add eggs and beat well; stir in juices. Chill for 3 hours. Just before serving, add ginger ale; pour mixture into a punch bowl and add scoops of sherbet. Makes about 24 half-cup servings.

MULLED CRANBERRY DRINK

1   12-ounce package fresh
    cranberries
8   cups (2 quarts) water
1½ cups sugar
2   tablespoons orange zest
6   cinnamon sticks
12 whole cloves
4   cups orange juice
1   cup lemon juice
    Thin lemon slices

Combine cranberries, water, sugar, orange zest, cinnamon sticks, and cloves in a large pot and cook over medium heat until cranberries are soft, about 15 minutes. Cranberries may start to pop. Strain mixture, then stir in juices. Warm mixture without letting it boil. Keep warm until ready to serve. Float a thin lemon slice in each cup. Makes 24 half-cup servings.

FROSTY FRAPPE FOR A CROWD

1   gallon pineapple sherbet
3   10-ounce packages frozen
        raspberries
1½   cups frozen blueberries
1½   cups frozen boysenberries
4 or 5 bananas, peeled and mashed
½ to 1 (2-liter) bottle lemon-lime soda

Soften sherbet and partially thaw raspberries, blueberries, and boysenberries. Spoon sherbet into a large bowl. Add partially thawed fruits and mashed bananas and stir just until blended. Stir in lemon-lime soda a little at a time to maintain the slushy consistency. Serve immediately by spooning into punch cups. Makes 32 servings.

FIESTA CRUSH

4   cups sugar
6   cups water
5   ripe bananas, peeled and mashed
2½ cups orange juice
4   cups pineapple juice
½   cup lemon juice
2   12-ounce cans lemon-lime soda
    Maraschino cherries, for
    garnishing

Combine sugar and water in a large saucepan and heat over medium heat until sugar is dissolved. Set aside to cool. In a large bowl, mash bananas, then stir in orange juice, pineapple juice, lemon juice, and cooled sugar syrup. Pour mixture into a shallow pan and freeze. When ready to serve, remove from freezer to thaw slightly. Break mixture into chunks and fill cups two-thirds full. Pour lemon-lime soda over slush. Garnish each serving with a maraschino cherry or sprig of holly. Makes 25 half-cup servings.

LIME SLUSH PUNCH

2   cups sugar

8   cups water

1   12-ounce can frozen limeade

5   fresh limes, juiced (about ½ cup)

2   12-ounce cans lemon-lime soda

Combine sugar and water in a large saucepan and heat until sugar is dissolved. Remove from heat and stir in frozen limeade and lime juice. Pour mixture into a shallow pan and freeze. (This slush can be kept in the freezer up to three months.) Remove mixture from freezer an hour before serving and break up with a fork until slushy. Pour into punch bowl and add lemon-lime soda. Makes 18 half-cup servings.

RASPBERRY SLUSH FOR A CROWD

3   packets unsweetened raspberry punch powder

4   cups sugar

4   cups warm water

1   46-ounce can pineapple juice

1   12-ounce can frozen lemonade concentrate

1   6-ounce can frozen lemon juice

3   20-ounce bags frozen raspberries

1   2-liter bottle lemon-lime soda

In a 3-gallon container, dissolve raspberry punch powder and sugar in warm water. Add pineapple juice, lemonade concentrate, lemon juice, frozen raspberries, and enough water (about 3½ quarts) to make 2 gallons punch. Stir until blended. Pour mixture into large freezer containers and freeze. When ready to serve, thaw mixture until slushy. Pour mixture into punch bowl or individual punch cups and add lemon-lime soda. Makes 75 half-cup servings.

GRAPE SPARKLE

2   cups sugar

4   cups water

2   cups grape juice

2   cups orange juice

½   cup lemon juice

1   12-ounce can ginger ale

Combine sugar and water in a large saucepan and heat over medium heat until sugar is dissolved. Remove from heat and let mixture cool. Stir in grape juice, orange juice, and lemon juice. Pour mixture into a shallow pan and freeze. When ready to serve, remove from freezer and thaw slightly. Break mixture into chunks and fill punch cups two-thirds full. Pour a small amount of ginger ale over slush and serve. Makes 20 half-cup servings.

Raspberry Slush for a Crowd

HOLLY BERRY SLUSH

2 cups sugar

2½ cups water

1 10-ounce bag frozen raspberries

1 cup orange juice

1 20-ounce can crushed pineapple, undrained

¼ cup lemon juice
Red food coloring (optional)

1 12-ounce can lemon-lime soda

Combine sugar and water in a large saucepan and heat over medium heat until sugar is dissolved. Remove from heat and stir in frozen raspberries. Add orange juice, crushed pineapple with juice, lemon juice, and a few drops of red food coloring, if desired. Pour mixture into a shallow pan and freeze. Remove mixture from freezer one hour before serving; break up with a fork until slushy. Fill punch cups two-thirds full with slush. Pour a small amount of lemon-lime soda over slush. Makes 20 half-cup servings.

SANTA CLAUS PUNCH

2 packets unsweetened raspberry punch powder

1 cup sugar

4 cups cranberry juice cocktail

12 cups (3 quarts) crushed ice and water

Combine raspberry punch powder with sugar in a large bowl; add cranberry juice cocktail and stir until powder and sugar are dissolved. Mix in crushed ice and water. Makes 32 half-cup servings.

FRUIT PUNCH CONCENTRATE

9 cups sugar

6 packets unsweetened orange punch powder

6 packets unsweetened cherry punch powder

1 46-ounce can orange juice

1 46-ounce can pineapple juice

Combine sugar and punch powders in a large container. Add orange juice and pineapple juice and stir until powder is dissolved. Store in refrigerator. When ready to serve, mix one part concentrate to four parts water. Makes 5 gallons when diluted.

HOT TOMATO ZIP

1   46-ounce can tomato juice
1   46-ounce can vegetable juice
      cocktail
2   10-ounce cans beef consommé
1   10-ounce can tomato soup
1   10-ounce soup can water
1   teaspoon seasoned salt
½   teaspoon onion salt
      Thin lemon slices, for garnishing

Combine all ingredients, except lemon slices, in a large saucepan and heat over medium heat. Serve warm, garnished with lemon slices. Makes 32 half-cup servings.

SHRIMP COCKTAIL BEVERAGE

2   46-ounce cans tomato juice
1½   cups ketchup
1   cup finely chopped celery
3   tablespoons sugar
2   4½-ounce cans cleaned, broken
      shrimp, drained
3   tablespoons Worcestershire sauce
2   tablespoons prepared horseradish
      sauce
      Juice of 1 lemon
½   teaspoon salt
½   teaspoon garlic salt

Combine all ingredients in a gallon container. Refrigerate several hours or overnight. Serve cold. Makes 25 half-cup servings.

HOT CRAB BITES

9   slices white bread
1   cup crabmeat or imitation crab,
      flaked
1   small onion, grated
1   cup grated cheddar cheese
1   cup mayonnaise
½   teaspoon salt
    Sliced olives and parsley sprigs, for
      garnishing

Remove crust from bread slices and set aside. In a large bowl, combine crabmeat, onion, cheese, mayonnaise, and salt. Spread mixture on bread slices. Cut each slice into fourths, in strips, squares, or triangles. Place pieces on a cookie sheet sprayed with cooking spray. Broil until crab topping is bubbly and golden. Garnish each piece with an olive slice and a sprig of parsley. Makes 36 appetizers.

SHRIMP PLATTER APPETIZER

1   8-ounce package cream cheese,
      softened
½   cup sour cream
¼   cup mayonnaise
2   4½-ounce cans shrimp, broken,
      rinsed, and drained
1   cup seafood cocktail sauce
2   cups grated mozzarella cheese
1   green pepper, chopped
3   green onions, chopped
1   large tomato, diced

Combine cream cheese, sour cream, and mayonnaise in a small bowl. Spread mixture on a 12-inch glass plate. Scatter shrimp over cream cheese layer. Cover with cocktail sauce. Add a layer of grated mozzarella cheese, a layer of green peppers, and a layer of green onions. Arrange diced tomato in the center. Cover with plastic wrap and chill. Serve with assorted crackers. Makes 12 to 16 servings.

CHICKEN ALMOND PUFFS

½ cup butter or margarine
1 cup chicken broth
1 cup flour
¼ teaspoon salt
4 eggs
1 cup finely diced cooked chicken
3 tablespoons finely chopped almonds

Preheat oven to 400 degrees. In a medium saucepan, heat butter and chicken stock over medium heat. When butter is melted, add flour and salt, and stir vigorously with a wooden spoon until mixture forms ball. Remove from heat. Beat eggs in, one at a time, and continue beating until eggs are incorporated and dough begins to stick to the edges of the pan. Stir in chicken and almonds. Drop by teaspoons onto greased baking sheet. Bake 15 minutes or until brown. Makes 4 dozen cocktail puffs.

SWEET AND SOUR CHICKEN STRIPS

8 boneless chicken breasts, skinned and sliced on the diagonal into ½-inch strips
1 egg
1½ cups cold water
1 cup flour, plus additional flour for coating chicken
½ cup cornstarch
1 teaspoon baking powder
½ teaspoon salt
¼ teaspoon black pepper
2 to 3 cups vegetable shortening, for deep-fat frying
1 cup sugar
2 tablespoons cornstarch
½ cup cider vinegar
½ cup ketchup
1 8-ounce can crushed pineapple, undrained
1 cup pineapple juice

Make tempura batter by beating egg and water in a medium bowl. Beat in 1 cup flour, ½ cup cornstarch, baking powder, salt, and pepper.

Put additional flour in a shallow bowl. Dip chicken strips in flour, then in batter.

Melt shortening in a large saucepan over medium-high heat. Once oil reaches 375 degrees on an instant-read thermometer, carefully add battered chicken strips to hot oil and fry for 2 to 3 minutes. When strips are golden brown, remove from oil with long tongs and place on paper towels to drain.

Make sweet and sour sauce by mixing sugar and 2 tablespoons cornstarch in a small saucepan; stir in remaining ingredients. Cook over medium heat and stir until thickened. Serve sauce as a dip for chicken strips. Makes 8 to 10 servings.

Glazed Meatballs

GLAZED MEATBALLS

3 slices bread (white or wheat)
⅔ cup milk
2 eggs, beaten well
1½ pounds ground beef
1 tablespoon Dijon mustard
½ teaspoon salt
½ teaspoon pepper
1 recipe Sweet-Sour Glaze or
   Swedish Meatball Sauce
   (see below)
   Hot, fluffy cooked rice (optional)

Note: To save time, you can use pre-cooked meatballs, which are available at your local grocery store. You can also use your favorite gravy in place of the glaze or sauce.

Preheat oven to 450 degrees. In a large bowl, soak bread slices in milk until soft. Add eggs, ground beef, and seasonings; mix until well blended. Shape mixture into ¾-inch or 1-inch balls; place meatballs on shallow baking sheets and bake 10 to 15 minutes. (Meatballs may be made to this point and then refrigerated until shortly before serving time.)

Pour Sweet-Sour Glaze or Swedish Meatball Sauce in a large pan; add meatballs and warm over medium heat. Serve in a chafing dish with toothpicks to spear the meatballs, or as a main course with hot, fluffy rice. Makes about 100 ¾-inch or 50 1-inch meatballs (25 servings).

Sweet-Sour Glaze

1½ cups chicken broth
¾ cup pineapple chunks
2 green peppers, cut in chunks
4 tablespoons cornstarch
1 tablespoon soy sauce
¾ cup rice vinegar
¾ cup sugar

Heat chicken broth, pineapple chunks, and green pepper chunks in a medium saucepan over medium heat; simmer 5 minutes. Stir in remaining ingredients. Cook and stir until thickened, approximately 1 minute.

Swedish Meatball Sauce

1 10½-ounce can cream of
   chicken soup
1 10½-ounce can cream of
   mushroom soup
1 soup can water

Combine all ingredients in a medium saucepan and heat over medium heat until warm.

SANDWICH ROLLS

1   large loaf sliced white
      sandwich bread
1   6½-ounce can tuna, drained
¼   cup minced celery
2   green onions, minced
1   tablespoon sweet pickle relish
¼   cup mayonnaise, plus additional
      mayonnaise for garnishing
      sandwiches
      Butter or margarine, softened
½   cup chopped fresh parsley
1   3-ounce package cream cheese,
      softened and divided
      Green and yellow food coloring

Trim crusts from bread to make 4x4-inch slices; set aside. In a large bowl, combine tuna, celery, green onions, pickle relish, and ¼ cup mayonnaise until well blended.

Flatten bread slices with a rolling pin, then spread with butter or margarine, followed by a thin layer of filling. Roll each slice into a tight roll.

Place additional mayonnaise in a small bowl and chopped parsley in another bowl. Dip sandwich ends in mayonnaise and then in chopped parsley. Place each roll, seam down, on a tray.

Tint half of the cream cheese yellow and the other half green. Fill pastry bags with tinted cream cheese and decorate the top of each sandwich with a flower and leaf, using star and leaf tips. Cover sandwiches with plastic wrap or store in a covered container and refrigerate until ready to serve. Makes 25 sandwich rolls.

BACON-CHESTNUT TIDBITS

1   pound bacon
2   8-ounce cans whole water chestnuts
1   cup ketchup
½   cup sugar

Preheat oven to 375 degrees. Cut each bacon strip into four pieces. Wrap each piece of bacon around a water chestnut and secure with a toothpick. Place skewers on a cookie sheet and bake for 10 minutes. Drain off fat and place bacon-wrapped tidbits in casserole dish. Combine ketchup and sugar and pour over top of tidbits. Cover and bake 15 minutes more. Makes 72 pieces.

Variation: In place of ketchup and sugar mixture, use favorite commercial or homemade barbecue sauce.

MARINATED MUSHROOMS

1   pound fresh button mushrooms
1   cup vinegar
1   cup vegetable oil
2   cloves garlic, minced
3   tablespoons minced fresh parsley
3   tablespoons minced green onion
1   teaspoon sugar
1   teaspoon salt

Clean and dry mushrooms. Stir remaining ingredients together until blended and pour over mushrooms. Cover and marinate in refrigerator overnight. When ready to serve, drain off marinade. Serve as appetizer or spoon on top of salad greens and serve as a salad. Makes 4 to 6 servings.

BROILED MUSHROOM APPETIZERS

Crab Filling

- 1   pound fresh button mushrooms
- 2   tablespoons margarine
- 1   7½-ounce can crabmeat, drained and flaked
- 1   cup mashed potatoes
- 1   cup grated cheddar cheese
- 2   teaspoons lemon juice
- 1   teaspoon seasoned salt

Clean mushrooms and air dry on paper towels. Remove stems. Chop stems into a small dice and sauté in 2 tablespoons margarine over medium-high heat for 2 to 3 minutes. Remove from heat and stir in remaining ingredients, mixing well. Spoon enough mixture to fill each mushroom cap (amount will vary depending on size of mushroom cap). Place on baking sheet and broil until lightly browned. Makes about 30 appetizers.

Bacon-Chive Filling

- ½   pound fresh mushrooms
- ½   pound bacon
- 2 to 3   tablespoons cream cheese, softened
- 2   tablespoons minced green onion

Clean mushrooms and remove stems. Discard stems or use for another purpose. Sauté bacon until brown and crisp; drain and crumble. Combine bacon, cream cheese, and green onion in a small bowl. Fill mushroom caps with mixture and place on baking sheet. Broil until lightly browned. Makes about 15 appetizers.

Onion-Cheese Filling

- ½   pound fresh mushrooms
- 1   3-ounce package cream cheese, softened
- 3   tablespoons fine dry bread crumbs
- 2   tablespoons finely chopped fresh parsley
- 2   teaspoons freshly grated onion
- ¼   teaspoon paprika
- ¼   teaspoon salt

Clean mushrooms and remove stems. Discard stems or use for another purpose. Combine remaining ingredients in a small bowl and fill each mushroom cap. Place mushroom caps on a baking sheet and broil until lightly browned. Makes about 15 appetizers.

PARTY DEVILED EGGS

6 hard-cooked eggs
1/4 cup mayonnaise
1 teaspoon vinegar
1 teaspoon prepared mustard
1/8 teaspoon salt
   Dash white pepper
1/8 teaspoon Worcestershire sauce
   Drop red pepper sauce (optional)
   Paprika, pimientos, and parsley,
      for garnishing

Peel eggs and cut in half lengthwise. Slip out yolks; mash with fork in a small bowl. Add remaining ingredients to yolks and mix until well blended. Spoon mixture into egg-white halves. Sprinkle with paprika and garnish with pimiento and parsley, if desired. Makes 12 deviled eggs.

LIVER PÂTÉ

1 pound pork liver
3/4 pound pork sausage
1 onion
2 tablespoons butter
2 tablespoons flour
2 cups milk
1 1/2 teaspoons salt
3/4 teaspoon pepper
1/2 teaspoon ground allspice
1/4 teaspoon ground cloves
2 eggs
   Pickled beets, for garnishing

Preheat oven to 350 degrees. Put liver, pork sausage, and onion through a meat grinder two times. Set aside while preparing white sauce.

Melt butter in a medium saucepan over medium-high heat; stir in flour, then milk, and cook, stirring constantly, until thickened.

Add white sauce to ground liver mixture and mix well. Stir in seasonings and eggs and mix well. Pour mixture into a greased, 5x9-inch loaf pan. Place loaf pan in a shallow pan of water and bake 1 1/4 hours. Cool. Remove from pan. Spread pâté on bread or crackers and garnish with a piece of pickled beet.

GUACAMOLE

2 large ripe avocados
1 tablespoon finely chopped green
      onion
1/2 teaspoon salt
   Dash oregano
1 1/2 tablespoons lemon juice
   Few drops red pepper sauce
      (optional)
   Chopped jalapeño peppers
      (optional)

Skin avocados and remove pits. Place in small bowl and mash with a fork. Add green onion, salt, and oregano; mash together thoroughly. Add lemon juice and mix again. For hot guacamole, add red pepper sauce or jalapeño peppers according to taste. Makes about 1 1/3 cups.

SALSA

- 2 cups chopped tomatoes
- ½ cup chopped onion
- 1 4-ounce can diced green chilies
- 1 clove garlic, minced
- ½ teaspoon salt
- ¼ teaspoon black pepper
- ¼ teaspoon cumin
- 1 tablespoon vinegar
- ¼ teaspoon crushed hot red pepper (optional)

Mix all ingredients in a medium bowl until well blended. Cover and refrigerate for at least 2 hours before serving. Or place all ingredients in blender and process for just a few seconds. The salsa should still be a little chunky, not smooth. Can be refrigerated for up to 1 week. Makes 3 cups.

TANGY PARTY DIP

- 1 8-ounce package cream cheese, softened
- ¼ cup mayonnaise
- ½ teaspoon red pepper sauce
- 1 teaspoon Worcestershire sauce
- 4 green onions, finely chopped
- 1 teaspoon seasoned salt
- ½ teaspoon paprika
- 1 3½-ounce package thinly sliced beef

In a small bowl, whip cream cheese and mayonnaise with electric mixer on low speed. Stir in seasonings. Finely chop the sliced beef and blend into cream-cheese mixture. Serve as a dip for fresh vegetables or as a spread for crackers. Makes 1¼ cups.

DILLY DIP

- 1 cup sour cream
- 1 cup mayonnaise
- 1 teaspoon Worcestershire sauce
- 1 tablespoon dill weed
- 1 tablespoon chopped green onion
- 1 tablespoon Bon Appetit®

In a medium bowl, mix all ingredients until well blended. Cover and refrigerate several hours or overnight. Makes 2 cups. Serve with fresh vegetables.

VEGETABLE CURRY DUNK

- 1 cup sour cream
- 1 cup mayonnaise
- ¼ cup finely chopped green onion
- ¼ cup chopped green peppers
- 2 tablespoons grated carrot
- 2 teaspoons curry powder
- ¼ teaspoon black pepper

Blend all ingredients in food processor or blender until smooth; chill for several hours. Makes 2½ cups dip. Serve with fresh vegetables.

Festive Cheese Ball

FESTIVE CHEESE BALL

- 2 8-ounce packages cream cheese, softened
- 2 cups grated sharp cheddar cheese
- 2 tablespoons finely chopped green onion
- 2 teaspoons Worcestershire sauce
- 1 teaspoon lemon juice
- 1/2 teaspoon lemon pepper
- 1 cup finely chopped nuts
- 1/2 cup chopped parsley

Combine all ingredients, except nuts and parsley, in a medium bowl and mix until well blended. Divide the mixture in half and spoon into 2 small bowls lined with waxed paper. Refrigerate for several hours. Lift out waxed paper from each bowl, and mold cheese into a ball, using waxed paper to protect hands. Roll each ball in chopped nuts and parsley. Refrigerate. Remove about 15 minutes before serving; serve with a variety of crackers. Makes 2 small cheese balls.

PINEAPPLE CHEESE ROLL

- 2 8-ounce packages cream cheese, softened
- 1 8 1/2-ounce can crushed pineapple, drained well
- 2 tablespoons finely chopped green onion
- 1/4 cup minced green pepper
- 1 tablespoon seasoned salt
- 1 cup chopped pecans

In a large bowl, combine cream cheese, pineapple, onions, green pepper, and seasoned salt. Mix well with a wooden spoon and refrigerate for several hours. Once firm and chilled, shape mixture into a log and roll in chopped pecans. Refrigerate until ready to serve. Makes 1 roll.

FRUIT DIP

- 2 8-ounce packages cream cheese, softened
- 1 16-ounce jar marshmallow crème
- 2 tablespoons frozen orange juice concentrate
- 1 teaspoon minced fresh ginger (optional)

Using an electric mixer, whip softened cream cheese with marshmallow crème and orange juice concentrate in a medium bowl until fluffy. Fold in fresh ginger, if desired. Use as a dip for fresh fruit. Makes 20 servings.

HONEY YOGURT DIP

- 1 16-ounce carton cottage cheese
- 1/2 cup plain yogurt
- 1/4 cup honey
- 1/2 cup grated coconut
- 2 teaspoons orange zest

Blend cottage cheese and yogurt in a food processor or blender until smooth. Stir in remaining ingredients; chill approximately 1 hour. Serve as a dip for fresh fruit. Makes 20 servings.

French Onion Soup

FRENCH ONION SOUP

3 cups sliced onions
¼ cup butter
2 cups beef stock (or 2 cups water and 2 tablespoons beef soup base)
2 cups chicken stock (or 2 cups water and 2 tablespoons chicken soup base)
1 teaspoon salt
¼ teaspoon pepper
1 recipe Parmesan Toast Cubes (see below)

In a medium saucepan, sauté sliced onions in melted butter until golden brown. Add beef stock, chicken stock, salt, and pepper. Simmer for 30 minutes. Ladle into bowls and top with Parmesan Toast Cubes just before serving. Makes 4 servings.

Parmesan Toast Cubes

1 loaf French bread
  Butter, room temperature
  Parmesan cheese, grated

Slice French bread into thick slices and place on a large baking sheet Spread each slice with enough softened butter to cover each slice. Sprinkle liberally with Parmesan cheese. Place slices under broiler and toast until light brown. Remove and cut into large cubes.

HEARTY TURKEY VEGETABLE SOUP

2 quarts Turkey Broth (see below)
1 cup cubed potatoes
1 cup sliced carrots
1 cup sliced celery
¼ cup chopped onions
1 teaspoon salt
  Pepper to taste
1 cup uncooked egg noodles
2 cups chopped cooked turkey meat
1 cup frozen peas

Add turkey broth, potatoes, carrots, celery, onions, salt, and pepper to a large soup pot. Bring to a boil over medium-high heat. Add noodles, reduce heat, and simmer 30 minutes. Stir in turkey and frozen peas; heat thoroughly and serve. Makes 8 servings.

Turkey Broth

1 roasted turkey
1 small carrot, sliced
1 small onion, chopped
  Celery leaves
2 teaspoons salt
1 bay leaf

Strip as much turkey meat as possible from bones of roasted turkey; refrigerate meat for later use in soup. Place bones and skin into a large stock pot and barely cover with water. Add carrot, chopped onion, a few celery leaves, salt, and bay leaf. Bring to a simmer over medium heat. Reduce heat, cover, and simmer for 2 to 3 hours. Strain broth, discarding carcass and other solids. Use broth immediately or refrigerate and use within 2 days. You may also freeze broth for 3 to 6 months.

Hearty Turkey Vegetable Soup

Chicken Dumpling Soup

CHICKEN DUMPLING SOUP

1   large onion, diced

2   carrots, diced

1½   stalks celery, diced

      Meat from 1 roasted chicken, cooked and shredded

4 to 6   cups chicken broth

1   cup fresh cut green beans

1   cup pearl barley, if desired

1   teaspoon celery salt

1   tablespoon fresh chopped parsley

1   bay leaf

1   teaspoon dried thyme

      Salt and pepper

1   recipe Dumpling Dough (see below)

Lightly sauté the onion, carrots, and celery in a small amount of oil in a large soup pot. Add shredded chicken, broth, green beans, pearl barley, celery salt, parsley, bay leaf, and thyme and simmer until the barley is tender. Season to taste with salt and pepper. Add spoon-sized balls of Dumpling Dough and simmer until dumplings rise. Makes enough for the whole family and friends if they stop by.

Dumpling Dough

1   cup milk

½   cup butter

½   teaspoon salt

½   teaspoon ground nutmeg

1   cup flour

3   eggs

Bring milk and butter to a boil in a medium saucepan; add salt and nutmeg. Remove from heat and immediately add flour, stirring until dough leaves the sides of the pan. Incorporate the eggs, one at a time, forming a sticky dough.

CHICKEN AND RICE SOUP

1   2½- to 3-pound fryer chicken
4   cups water
1   carrot, cut in chunks
1   onion, cut in chunks
1   celery stalk, cut in chunks
1   teaspoon salt
1   clove garlic, crushed
1   cup cooked rice
2   fresh tomatoes, cut into wedges
½   cup chopped green pepper
1   medium onion, chopped
1   cup frozen peas
¼   cup sliced pimiento-stuffed olives

Place chicken, water, carrot, onion, celery, salt, and garlic in a large soup pot. Bring to a slow boil and then reduce heat to simmer. Cover and simmer for 1 hour. Remove chicken from broth and set aside to cool slightly. Strain vegetables from broth and discard; set broth aside to cool. Once chicken is cool enough to handle, remove bones and skin. Cut chicken into bite-sized pieces.

Skim the fat off the broth and return to stove top. Stir in cut-up chicken, rice, tomatoes, green pepper, chopped onion, frozen peas, and olives. Heat, uncovered, until hot and onion and peppers are tender, about 10 minutes. Makes 8 servings.

TACO SOUP

1   tablespoon vegetable oil
1   cup chopped onion
1   pound ground beef
1   package mild taco seasoning mix
2   cups frozen corn
1   16-ounce can kidney beans, drained and rinsed
1   28-ounce can stewed tomatoes
1   8-ounce can tomato sauce
2   cups water
    Tortilla chips
    Grated cheese

In a large soup pot, sauté onions in vegetable oil until softened. Place sautéed onions in a bowl and set aside. Brown ground beef in the same pot; drain off fat. Stir in sautéed onions, taco seasoning, corn, kidney beans, stewed tomatoes, tomato sauce, and water. Bring to a simmer over medium heat and let simmer for 20 to 30 minutes. Serve topped with tortilla chips and grated cheese. Makes 8 servings.

Patrick's Gumbo Soup

1/4 cup butter

3 large yellow onions, diced

2 large red bell peppers, diced

2 stalks celery, diced

1 12-ounce can diced tomatoes, undrained

1 8-ounce can diced green chilies, undrained

2 cups clam juice

1 cup tomato juice

4 cups water

1 1/2 cups canned black beans, rinsed

1/2 pound salad shrimp

1/4 cup rice

1/2 pound pork sausage

1/2 teaspoon minced garlic

1 teaspoon cayenne pepper

2 tablespoons paprika

1/2 cup brown sugar

1 1/2 teaspoons salt

3 cups frozen sliced okra

Melt butter in a large soup pot over medium-high heat. Add onions, peppers, and celery and sauté until tender. Stir in tomatoes and chilies, with liquid from both. Add clam juice, tomato juice, and water; bring to a boil. Stir in beans, shrimp, and rice. Reduce to medium heat and simmer. While soup simmers, brown sausage in a medium skillet; drain off fat. Add sausage, seasonings, and okra to other ingredients. Cook until rice is tender. Makes 12 to 16 servings.

Warming Soups

Peasant Soup

1 cup Great Northern beans

1 teaspoon salt

1 ham hock (or ½ pound bacon or diced ham)

3 carrots, peeled and diced

1 onion, chopped

1 cup chopped celery

2 cups chopped cabbage

½ teaspoon garlic powder

½ teaspoon black pepper

1 tablespoon taco seasoning

Cover beans with water and soak overnight (or bring to a boil for 2 minutes, remove from heat, and let stand covered for 1 hour). Drain beans and combine with 3 cups water, salt, and ham hock in a large soup pot. Cover and simmer until beans are tender, about 2 hours. Add carrots, onion, celery, cabbage, remaining seasonings, and 4 cups water. Simmer covered until vegetables are tender. Remove ham hock and strip meat from bone. Dice meat and return to soup. Makes 8 servings.

Lion House Oyster Stew

3 tablespoons margarine

3 tablespoons flour

2 cups milk

2 cups light cream

2 8-ounce cans oysters and juice

½ teaspoon salt

¼ teaspoon black pepper

Make a roux by melting margarine in a heavy soup pot over medium-high heat until foamy. Stir in flour and cook until fragrant and golden brown. Reduce heat to medium. Gradually stir in milk and light cream, cooking and stirring until thickened. Add oysters with juice and seasonings. Heat slowly to simmer point; do not boil. Serve when oysters are hot. Makes 6 servings.

SEAFOOD BISQUE

1½ to 2 cups cooked fish (halibut, salmon, cod, or other)
½ cup cooked shrimp
¼ cup butter
½ cup diced celery
¼ cup minced green onion
3 tablespoons flour
2 cups milk
1 cup light cream
1 cup fish stock or clam juice
1 teaspoon salt
4 drops red pepper sauce
⅛ teaspoon black pepper
1 teaspoon savory salt
Minced parsley, for garnishing

Shred fish and shrimp with fork and set aside. Melt butter in a heavy soup pot over medium-high heat. Add celery and onion and sauté until softened. Stir in flour. Gradually add milk, cream, and fish stock or clam juice. Cook and stir over medium heat until slightly thickened. Add shredded fish, salt, red pepper sauce, pepper, and savory salt. Simmer for a few minutes to blend flavors; do not boil. Garnish each serving with minced parsley. Makes 6 servings.

BROCCOLI-CHEESE SOUP

1½ pounds fresh broccoli, chopped, or 2 10-ounce packages frozen chopped broccoli
3 tablespoons margarine
¼ cup chopped onion
3 tablespoons flour
2 cups chicken broth (or 2 cups water and 2 tablespoons chicken soup base)
2 cups light cream
1 teaspoon salt
¼ teaspoon nutmeg
1 cup grated cheddar cheese

Cook broccoli in small amount of salted water until tender; drain and set aside. Make a roux by melting margarine in a heavy soup pot over medium heat until margarine is foamy. Add onion and cook until translucent. Stir in flour. Slowly add broth and cream, cooking and stirring until thickened. Add salt, nutmeg, and cooked broccoli. Warm through. Just before serving, stir in cheese. Makes 6 servings.

Vegetable-Cheese Chowder

4 cups cubed potatoes

2 cups diced carrots

2 cups chopped celery

1/2 cup minced onions

2 teaspoons salt

4 cups water

1 10-ounce package frozen broccoli

3 tablespoons chicken soup base

3 1/2 cups milk

1/2 cup margarine

1/2 cup flour

1 tablespoon dry mustard

1 pound processed American cheese, cubed

Place potatoes, carrots, celery, and onions in a large soup pot and add salt and water. Cook over medium-high heat until vegetables are tender, about 20 minutes. Stir in broccoli, chicken soup base, and milk. Simmer for 5 more minutes. In a separate saucepan, make a roux by melting margarine over medium-high heat until foamy. Stir in flour and dry mustard and cook and stir until fragrant and golden brown, about 1 minute. Add roux to soup and stir until thickened. Add cheese to soup and stir until melted. Keep hot, without boiling, until ready to serve. Makes 8 to 10 servings.

Cream of Leek Soup

4 cups chicken stock (or 4 cups water and 1/4 cup chicken soup base)

3 large leeks (about 3 cups chopped)

1 cup chopped celery

1 cup chopped onions

6 potatoes, cooked, peeled, and cubed

1 bay leaf

1 teaspoon salt

  Black pepper to taste

3 cups milk

1/4 cup butter or margarine

1/2 cup flour

Heat chicken stock in large soup pot. Trim green tops from leeks within 2 inches of white part; discard tops. Wash leeks thoroughly and chop coarsely. Add leeks, celery, onions, potatoes, bay leaf, salt, and pepper to chicken stock and simmer until vegetables are tender. Stir in milk and heat through. In a separate saucepan, make a roux by melting butter or margarine over medium-high heat until foamy. Stir in flour and cook until golden brown and fragrant. Add roux to soup and stir until thickened. Makes 8 to 10 servings.

VICHYSSOISE

Follow recipe for Cream of Leek Soup (page 28). Press cooked vegetables and chicken stock through a sieve. Add 3 cups of half and half instead of milk. Season with ½ teaspoon nutmeg before thickening with roux. Chill several hours. Serve cold, garnished with unsweetened whipped cream and snipped chives. Makes 8 to 10 servings.

CREAM OF ASPARAGUS SOUP

1   15-ounce can asparagus,
        undrained*
3   tablespoons margarine
¼   cup minced onions
3   tablespoons flour
1   15-ounce can chicken broth
1   cup milk
¼   teaspoon paprika
½   teaspoon salt

Pour asparagus and its liquid into a blender and process until puréed; set aside. In a heavy soup pot, melt margarine over medium-high heat; add onions, and sauté until soft. Stir in flour. Add puréed asparagus, chicken broth, milk, paprika, and salt. Cook and stir until slightly thickened. Makes 6 servings.

*If using fresh asparagus, simmer ¾-pound fresh, cleaned asparagus in 2 cups salted water until tender. Remove asparagus from water. Cool slightly and purée in blender. Follow recipe as above.

Orange Fruit Slaw

ORANGE FRUIT SLAW

3   cups shredded cabbage
1   orange, peeled and sectioned
1   cup halved seedless red grapes
½   cup sliced celery
1   apple, cored and chopped
1   8-ounce carton orange yogurt
¼   cup toasted slivered almonds*

Combine cabbage, orange sections, grapes, celery, and apple in a large salad bowl. Mix in orange yogurt. Chill 2 to 3 hours. Just before serving, garnish with toasted slivered almonds.

*To toast almonds, spread on a baking sheet and place in a 350-degree oven for 5 to 8 minutes, stirring occasionally until lightly toasted.

LION HOUSE BUFFET SALAD

1   small head iceberg lettuce
1   small head romaine lettuce
2   large tomatoes, diced
2   avocados, diced
¼   cup chopped green onion
4   hard-cooked eggs, peeled and sliced
½   pound bacon, cooked crisp and
        crumbled
6   slices American processed cheese,
        sliced into thin strips
½   cup sliced black olives
1   cup Italian salad dressing

Wash lettuces and tear into bite-sized pieces into a large bowl. Add tomatoes, avocados, green onion, eggs, bacon, cheese, and olives. Keep chilled until ready to serve. Just before serving, add dressing and toss lightly to combine. Makes 8 to 10 servings.

POPPY SEED SPINACH TOSS

1 pound fresh spinach
½ head iceberg lettuce
1 cup grated Swiss cheese
1 cup cottage cheese or ricotta cheese
½ pound fresh mushrooms, cleaned and sliced
½ Bermuda onion, sliced thin and separated into rings
2 hard-cooked eggs, peeled and chopped
1 recipe Poppy Seed Dressing (see below)

Wash spinach, dry thoroughly, and discard stems. Tear in pieces into a large salad bowl. Tear lettuce in pieces into bowl. Add Swiss cheese, cottage cheese, mushrooms, onion rings, and chopped eggs. When ready to serve, pour Poppy Seed Dressing over salad and toss to coat greens. Serve immediately. Makes 8 servings.

Poppy Seed Dressing

½ cup red wine vinegar
¾ cup salad oil
2 teaspoons poppy seeds
4 tablespoons sugar
1 tablespoon minced Bermuda onion
1 teaspoon salt
½ teaspoon dry mustard

Pour vinegar and oil in blender. Add poppy seeds, sugar, minced Bermuda onion, salt, and dry mustard. Process until well blended. Or place ingredients in a pint jar and shake until oil is emulsified. Refrigerate. Flavor improves if dressing is made several hours in advance. Makes 1½ cups.

ORIENTAL CABBAGE SLAW WITH CHICKEN

2 cups diced cooked chicken
4 cups shredded cabbage
1 package chicken-flavored ramen noodles
1 quart boiling water
4 green onions, sliced
2 tablespoons sesame seeds
¼ cup vinegar
¼ cup salad oil
2 tablespoons sugar
½ teaspoon salt
1 flavoring packet from ramen noodles
½ cup slivered almonds

Place chicken and cabbage in large mixing bowl. Break noodles up and place in colander. Pour boiling water over noodles to soften slightly. Add softened noodles, onions, and sesame seeds to chicken and cabbage. In a separate bowl combine vinegar, oil, sugar, salt, and contents of flavoring packet. Pour over noodles and cabbage, mixing well. Cover and refrigerate overnight or for several hours. Just before serving, stir in slivered almonds. Makes 6 to 8 servings.

Poppy Seed Spinach Toss

Sugar Pea Salad

Sugar Pea Salad

1¼ pounds sugar peas
1 cup fresh mushrooms, sliced thin
½ cup finely chopped red bell pepper
1 cup bean sprouts, rinsed and
   drained
8 ounces cooked shrimp
¼ cup olive oil
1 tablespoon soy sauce
2 tablespoons lemon juice
1 teaspoon brown sugar
   Leaf lettuce, for garnishing
2 tablespoons sesame seeds

Cut blossom end from peapods and place in bowl; add mushrooms, red bell pepper, bean sprouts, and shrimp. In a separate bowl combine olive oil, soy sauce, lemon juice, and brown sugar. Pour over vegetables and stir to coat. Cover and refrigerate for several hours, stirring occasionally. To serve, spoon onto lettuce leaf and sprinkle with sesame seeds. Makes 6 to 8 servings.

Rice-Shrimp Salad

2 cups water
1 cup uncooked rice
1 teaspoon salt
2 cups cooked salad shrimp
1 small can pimientos, diced
2 tablespoons chopped green onion
1 small green pepper, chopped
1 small carrot, chopped
1 10-ounce package frozen green
   peas, cooked and drained
1 cup mayonnaise
1 teaspoon seasoned salt
¼ teaspoon pepper
   Leaf lettuce, for garnishing

Bring water, rice, and salt to a boil in a medium saucepan; cover and reduce heat to low. Let sit for about 20 minutes. Remove from heat, fluff rice with a fork, and let cool. Once cooled, combine cooked rice with remaining ingredients until well blended. Cover and refrigerate for several hours or overnight. To serve, scoop mixture onto individual lettuce leaves. Makes 6 to 8 servings

FIVE-WAY CRAB SALAD

8 ounces imitation crabmeat

½ cup sliced celery

¼ cup chopped green onion

1 tomato, cubed

¼ cup sliced ripe olives

3 hard-cooked eggs, peeled and chopped

½ cup mayonnaise

½ teaspoon seasoned salt

½ teaspoon prepared mustard

Salt and pepper to taste

Combine crabmeat with celery, onions, tomato, olives, and chopped eggs. Gently blend in mayonnaise and seasonings. Chill. Makes 4 to 5 cups salad. Serve in any of the following ways:

Stuffed Avocado—Cut 4 avocados in half; remove pits. Scoop crab salad into center of cavity. Makes 8 stuffed avocados.

Stuffed Tomato—Cut 6 to 8 tomatoes into 8 sections, leaving connected at bottom. Place each tomato on lettuce leaf and scoop crab salad into center of each. Fills 6 to 8 tomatoes.

Croissant Sandwiches—Slice croissants and stuff with crab salad. Makes 6 to 8 croissant sandwiches.

Crab Puffs—Cut tops off cocktail-size cream puffs. Spoon crab salad into each puff and garnish with sprig of parsley. Fills 20 to 24 puffs.

Entrée Salad—Line 6 large salad plates with green leafy lettuce. Place mound of shredded lettuce in center. Spoon crab salad on top of shredded lettuce. Garnish with lemon wedge, olives, tomato wedges, and parsley. Makes 6 large salads.

TORTELLINI PRIMAVERA

1 8-ounce package tortellini

2 stalks broccoli, cut into flowerets

3 carrots, peeled and sliced

½ cup chopped green onion

½ cup chopped red pepper

½ cup chopped green pepper

½ cup mayonnaise

1 teaspoon orange zest

½ teaspoon dried thyme

1 teaspoon dried basil

1 teaspoon salt

¼ teaspoon black pepper

Leaf lettuce, for garnishing

½ cup grated mozzarella cheese, for garnishing

Cook tortellini in boiling, salted water about 15 minutes or until tender. Drain and cool under cold running water; set aside. Steam broccoli and sliced carrots until crisp-tender. Cool under cold running water. In a large bowl combine tortellini, broccoli, carrots, green onions, and red and green peppers. In a separate bowl, mix mayonnaise, orange zest, and seasonings. Pour over tortellini mixture and toss to coat.

For each serving, line a salad plate with lettuce. Spoon on a mound of salad mixture. Sprinkle with 1 tablespoon grated cheese. Serve chilled or at room temperature. Makes 8 servings.

Five-Way Crab Salad

Seafood Pasta Salad

8 ounces pasta spirals
2 cups diced provolone or cheddar cheese
2 small carrots, thinly sliced
1 small zucchini, quartered and sliced
1 cup sliced mushrooms
¾ cup bias-cut celery
½ cup thinly sliced radishes
¼ cup chopped red onion
1 small green pepper, cut in 1-inch strips
½ cup black olives, cut in half
2 cups imitation crabmeat
1 7-ounce carton clam dip
Salt and pepper to taste

Cook pasta according to package directions; drain and chill. Combine chilled pasta, cheese, carrots, zucchini, mushrooms, celery, radishes, red onion, green pepper, and olives in a large bowl. Add crabmeat and clam dip; mix until well blended. Stir in salt and pepper to taste. Refrigerate until ready to serve. Makes 10 to 12 servings.

Christmas Eggnog Salad

1 ¼-ounce envelope unflavored gelatin
1 8-ounce can crushed pineapple, undrained
2 tablespoons lemon juice
1½ cups dairy eggnog
½ cup finely chopped celery
1½ cups cranberry juice cocktail or apple juice
1 3-ounce package raspberry gelatin
1 14-ounce jar (1¾ cups) cranberry-orange relish
Frosted cranberries, for garnishing*

In a medium saucepan, soften unflavored gelatin in undrained crushed pineapple for 5 minutes. Add lemon juice. Cook and stir over medium heat until gelatin dissolves. Stir in eggnog and celery and pour into a 12x7x2-inch pan. Chill until almost firm. In a medium saucepan bring cranberry juice to a boil. Remove from heat; add raspberry gelatin and stir until dissolved. Fold in cranberry-orange relish. Chill until partially set, pour over eggnog mixture. Chill until firm. Cut into squares. Garnish with frosted cranberries. Makes 12 servings.

* To frost cranberries, beat 1 egg white until fluffy. Add cranberries to egg white then spoon onto wire rack. Let egg whites drip off the berries. Sprinkle with granulated sugar. Air dry.

FRUIT SALAD FOR A CROWD

2   3.5-ounce packages instant pudding
    (coconut cream or pistachio)
1   20-ounce can crushed pineapple,
    undrained
1   20-ounce can pineapple tidbits,
    undrained
2   8-ounce cans mandarin oranges,
    drained
½   cup flaked coconut
2   cups red or green seedless grapes
2   cups miniature marshmallows
1   20-ounce carton frozen whipped
    topping, thawed

In a large bowl, mix instant pudding with crushed pineapple and pineapple tidbits, including their juices. Stir in remaining ingredients until well blended. Cover and refrigerate until ready to serve. Chill 2 to 3 hours. Makes 20 to 25 servings.

ORCHARD FRUIT SALAD

    Zest and juice of 1 orange
2   fresh pears, cored and cut into
    chunks
2   red apples, cored and cut into
    chunks
½   cup fresh or frozen raspberries or
    blackberries
¼   cup slivered almonds
    Leaf lettuce, for garnishing
    Flaked coconut, for garnishing

Toss orange zest, juice, pears, and apples together in a medium bowl. Gently fold in raspberries or blackberries and slivered almonds. When ready to serve, spoon fruit onto a lettuce leaf and sprinkle with coconut. Makes 4 to 6 servings.

STRAWBERRY NUT SALAD

1   6-ounce package strawberry
    gelatin
1   cup boiling water
1   10-ounce package frozen sliced
    strawberries, thawed but
    undrained
1   20-ounce can crushed pineapple,
    drained
3   medium bananas, peeled and mashed
½   cup walnuts, coarsely chopped
1   16-ounce carton sour cream

In a large bowl dissolve gelatin in boiling water. Fold in strawberries, pineapple, mashed bananas, and nuts. Pour one-half of mixture into an 8x12-inch pan. Refrigerate until firm. Stir sour cream until smooth, then spread on set gelatin. Gently spoon remainder of gelatin mixture (which has been at room temperature) on top. Refrigerate. Makes 8 to 10 servings.

Angie Earl's Frozen Fruit Salad

ANGIE EARL'S FROZEN FRUIT SALAD

- 1   pint whipping cream
- 1   cup mayonnaise
- ¼   cup powdered sugar
- 3   tablespoons lemon juice
- ¼   teaspoon salt
- ½   cup chopped nuts
- 1   cup crushed pineapple, drained
- ½   cup chopped maraschino cherries
- 1   cup fruit cocktail, drained
  Leaf lettuce, for garnishing

In a large bowl whip cream until stiff; blend in mayonnaise, powdered sugar, lemon juice, and salt. Pour mixture into a 4½ x 8½-inch loaf pan; place in freezer and partially freeze (about 2 hours). Remove from freezer, return to bowl, and fold in nuts, pineapple, maraschino cherries, and fruit cocktail. Pour back into loaf pan and freeze several days to ripen. To serve, scoop onto serving plates with an ice cream scoop, or cut into slices and serve on a lettuce leaf. Makes 8 servings.

MOLDED FRESH CRANBERRY SALAD

- 2   cups water
- ¾   cup sugar
- 1   12-ounce package fresh cranberries
- 1   6-ounce package orange gelatin
- 1   8.25-ounce can crushed pineapple, with juice
- ½   cup chopped celery
  Salad greens, for garnishing
- 1   8-ounce carton sour cream, for garnishing
- 8   orange slices, for garnishing

In a medium saucepan, bring water, sugar, and cranberries to a boil. Boil 5 minutes. Remove from heat and stir in gelatin until dissolved. Add crushed pineapple, including its juice, and celery. Pour into 8 single-serving-sized molds. Refrigerate until firm, at least 6 hours. Unmold on salad greens. Garnish each serving with a dollop of sour cream and an orange slice. Makes 8 servings.

CHRISTMAS RAINBOW SALAD

- 1   6-ounce package red gelatin
- 1   cup boiling water
- 1   cup ice water
- 1   15.25-ounce can crushed pineapple, undrained
- 1   6-ounce package lemon gelatin
- 1   cup boiling water
- 1   cup ice water
- ½   pint whipping cream, whipped stiff
- 1   3-ounce package lime gelatin
- 1   cup boiling water
- 1   cup ice water

Dissolve red gelatin in 1 cup boiling water. Mix in 1 cup ice water and crushed pineapple. Pour into a 9x13-inch pan or large mold and refrigerate until set.

Dissolve lemon gelatin in 1 cup boiling water. Add 1 cup ice water and refrigerate until syrupy. Whip until foamy, then fold in whipped cream and pour over red gelatin layer. Refrigerate until set.

Dissolve lime gelatin in 1 cup boiling water. Add 1 cup ice water. Pour over lemon layer. Refrigerate until set. Makes 12 servings.

Roast Turkey

ROAST TURKEY

To buy: When buying turkeys under 12 pounds, allow about ¾ pound per serving. For turkeys 12 pounds and over, allow about ½ pound per serving.

To thaw: If the turkey is frozen, leave in original bag and thaw in refrigerator for 3 to 4 days. Cook as soon as thawed.

To roast: Remove plastic wrap; remove giblets and neck from body cavities. Rinse turkey inside and out, and pat dry with paper towel. Stuff turkey just before roasting—not ahead of time. Fill wishbone area first. Fasten neck skin to back with skewer. Fold wings across back with tips touching. Fill body cavity lightly. Tuck drumsticks under band of skin at the tail or tie together with heavy string, then tie tail. Place turkey, breast-side up, on rack in shallow roasting pan. Roast uncovered at 325 degrees. Season turkey with favorite seasonings. When turkey begins to turn golden, cover with tent of foil to prevent over browning.

Approximate Cooking Times for Ready-to-Cook Turkey

8 to 12 pounds: 3 to 4½ hours

12 to 16 pounds: 4½ to 5½ hours

16 to 20 pounds: 5½ to 6½ hours

20 to 24 pounds: 6½ to 7½ hours

Internal Temperature: 185 degrees

To serve: Remove turkey from oven and allow to stand about 20 minutes. Use drippings for gravy. Remove stuffing from turkey. Carve and serve. Refrigerate leftovers as soon as possible after serving.

OLD-FASHIONED SAVORY STUFFING

4 cups diced celery
1 cup chopped onion
1 cup butter or margarine
4 quarts (16 cups) dry bread cubes
1 tablespoon salt
1½ teaspoons poultry seasoning
½ teaspoon sage
½ teaspoon pepper
¾ to 1 cup hot broth or water

Sauté celery and onion in butter in a large skillet. Combine with bread cubes and seasonings; toss lightly. Add enough broth to moisten as desired. Makes enough stuffing for a 14- to 18-pound bird.

Giblet Stuffing: Add chopped, cooked giblets; use giblet broth as liquid.

Oyster Stuffing: Add two 8-ounce cans oysters, drained and chopped.

Chestnut Stuffing: Add 1 pound fresh chestnuts. Prepare chestnuts by slashing shells with a sharp knife. Roast on baking sheet at 400 degrees for 15 minutes; cool. Peel and coarsely chop chestnuts; then add to stuffing.

PIONEER TURKEY BAKE

2 cups cubed cooked turkey
1 6-ounce package wild rice mix
½ cup chopped celery
2 tablespoons chopped onion
1 4-ounce can sliced mushrooms, drained
1 10-ounce can cream of chicken soup
1 teaspoon Worcestershire sauce
1¼ cups water
¼ cup slivered almonds

Preheat oven to 350 degrees. Combine turkey with wild rice mix, including contents of seasoning packet. Add remaining ingredients and mix well. Pour into a 1½-quart casserole. Bake covered for 45 minutes. Makes 6 servings.

HOT TURKEY SALAD SUPREME

2 cups diced cooked turkey
2 cups chopped celery
½ teaspoon salt
2 tablespoons minced onion
2 tablespoons lemon juice
1 cup mayonnaise
¾ cup grated cheddar cheese
1 cup crushed potato chips
½ cup slivered almonds
Leaf lettuce, for serving
Lemon wedges and parsley sprigs,
   for garnishing

Preheat oven to 350 degrees. Mix turkey, celery, salt, onion, and lemon juice in a medium bowl. Fold in mayonnaise and spoon into a greased casserole dish. Sprinkle grated cheese on top, followed by crushed potato chips and slivered almonds. Bake for 15 minutes. Don't overbake; mayonnaise will break down. Serve on lettuce leaves and garnish with lemon wedges and parsley. Makes 6 to 8 servings.

CHICKEN DIJON

4 boneless, skinless chicken breast
   halves
¼ cup water
¾ cup white grape juice
1 small onion, sliced
3 tablespoons lemon juice
1 chicken bouillon cube
12 whole peppercorns
1 teaspoon dried thyme
1 tablespoon honey
2 teaspoons Dijon mustard
1½ cups sliced fresh mushrooms
2 teaspoons flour
2 tablespoons water
4 sprigs fresh thyme, for garnishing
4 lemon slices, for garnishing

Place chicken breasts in a 12-inch skillet and add water, grape juice, onion slices, lemon juice, bouillon cube, peppercorns, and thyme. Cover and simmer 15 minutes or until chicken is no longer pink. Remove chicken and keep warm in serving dish. Strain pan liquids through a mesh sieve; discard solids and return liquid to pan. Add honey, mustard, and mushrooms. Bring to a boil and simmer 10 minutes. Make a paste of flour and water and stir into the sauce. Cook and stir over medium heat until slightly thickened. Spoon sauce over chicken. Garnish each breast with a sprig of thyme and a lemon slice, if desired. Makes 4 servings.

Chicken and Wild Rice

CHICKEN AND WILD RICE

6 to 8   boneless, skinless chicken breasts
6   cups flour
2   tablespoons chili powder
1   teaspoon cayenne pepper
1   teaspoon paprika
1   tablespoon salt
1½   teaspoons black pepper
4   cups milk
2   cups oil
1   recipe Sauce (see below)
1   recipe Wild Rice (see below)

Divide the flour in half and put in two separate bowls. In the first bowl add chili powder, cayenne, paprika, salt, and pepper. Mix well. Place raw chicken breasts into the other bowl and coat evenly with flour, making sure to remove any excess flour. Pour milk into a third bowl. Place chicken from flour into milk, one at a time. Remove and put each breast into seasoned flour to coat. Heat a large frying pan with oil on medium-high heat. Place each piece of meat in oil and cook approximately 2 minutes on each side or until golden brown. When browned, place chicken on a baking sheet in a 365-degree oven. Cook until internal temperature of chicken reaches 165 degrees on meat thermometer. Makes 6 servings.

Sauce

½   cup butter
1½   cup diced onions
¾   cup flour
8   cups milk
1½   teaspoons cayenne pepper
1   tablespoon paprika
½   teaspoon Worcestershire sauce
½   teaspoon Tabasco® sauce
1   lemon, juiced
    Salt and pepper to taste

Melt butter and sauté onions until translucent. Add flour and stir until smooth. Let cook until slightly browned (about 5 minutes). Add milk, cayenne, paprika, Worcestershire sauce, and Tabasco sauce. Simmer over medium heat until thickened. Add lemon juice and salt and pepper to taste. Pour over baked chicken just before serving.

Wild Rice

1   tablespoon butter
1   cup white rice
½   cup wild rice
3   cups water
½   teaspoon salt

Melt butter in saucepan. Add white and wild rice and stir over medium heat until white rice begins to brown. Add water and salt. Bring to a boil. Cover and reduce heat to low. Cook for 15 to 20 minutes or until tender. Serve with chicken. Makes 6 servings.

SAVORY BAKED CHICKEN BREASTS

1 cup sour cream

2 tablespoons lemon juice

8 boneless, skinless chicken breast halves

1 teaspoon salt

1 teaspoon seasoned salt

1½ teaspoons paprika

1½ teaspoons sage

1½ teaspoons garlic salt

½ teaspoon black pepper

3 cups fine bread crumbs

½ cup butter or margarine, melted

Note: Start this dish early in the day—or the night before serving—so chicken has time to soak up flavors from the simple marinade.

At least 4 hours before baking, combine sour cream and lemon juice in a small bowl. Place chicken breasts in a shallow bowl and pour mixture over chicken. Cover and refrigerate.

When ready to bake, preheat oven to 325 degrees and grease a 9x13-inch baking dish. Combine salt, seasoned salt, paprika, sage, garlic salt, and black pepper in a medium bowl. Mix in bread crumbs. Dip chicken breasts in crumb mixture to coat all sides. Arrange in baking pan. Drizzle melted butter over top. Cover with foil and bake for 2 hours. Remove foil and bake an additional 30 minutes to brown. Makes 8 servings.

SWEET AND SOUR CHICKEN

6 boneless, skinless chicken breasts

1 teaspoon garlic salt

½ teaspoon black pepper

1 tablespoon vegetable oil

1 egg, beaten well

4 to 6 tablespoons cornstarch or flour

¾ cup sugar

½ cup cider vinegar

½ cup chicken stock

3½ tablespoons ketchup

1 tablespoon soy sauce

Sprinkle chicken with garlic salt and pepper. Refrigerate for at least one hour. Preheat oven to 325 degrees. Heat oil in a 12-inch skillet over medium-high heat. Put beaten egg in a shallow dish; place cornstarch or flour in a shallow dish. Dip chicken in beaten egg, then in cornstarch or flour. Place chicken in hot oil and brown on both sides. Place chicken in baking dish and set aside.

Prepare sweet and sour sauce by mixing sugar, vinegar, chicken stock, ketchup, and soy sauce in a medium saucepan and heating until sugar is dissolved. Pour over chicken. Bake uncovered for 1 hour. Turn chicken once or twice during baking time. Makes 6 servings.

CHICKEN FAJITAS

- 6 boneless, skinless chicken breasts
- 1 cup water
- 1 package fajitas seasoning mix
- 2 tablespoons vegetable oil
- 2 onions, sliced
- 1 green pepper, sliced in strips
- 1 red pepper, sliced in strips
- 12 flour tortillas
  Sour cream, for garnishing
  Salsa, for garnishing (see page 15)
  Guacamole, for garnishing (see page 14)
  Limes, for garnishing

Cut chicken breasts into strips. Combine water and seasoning mix in a medium bowl and marinate strips for two hours. Heat oil in a 12-inch skillet over medium-high heat and sauté onions and peppers until crisp-tender. Remove vegetables from pan and set aside. Place chicken strips in pan, reserving marinade. Sauté chicken until light brown. Add leftover marinade to the pan and simmer for five minutes. Return vegetables to pan and heat to mingle flavors. Spoon mixture onto warm tortillas. Fold over and garnish with sour cream, salsa, guacamole, and a slice of fresh lime. Makes 6 servings.

CHICKEN CRÊPES

- 2 cups chopped cooked chicken
- ½ cup grated cheddar cheese
- 1 15-ounce can pineapple tidbits, drained (reserve juice)
- ½ cup chopped almonds
- 1 10-ounce can cream of chicken soup
- ½ cup reserved pineapple juice
- ½ teaspoon dried thyme
- ½ teaspoon lemon pepper
- 12 crêpes (see recipe on page 92)
- 1 recipe Chicken Glaze

Preheat oven to 200 degrees. Mix chicken, grated cheese, pineapple tidbits, and almonds with chicken soup and reserved pineapple juice in a large bowl. Add thyme and lemon pepper and mix thoroughly. Place ¼ cup of the mixture in center of each crepe and roll. Place crepes with seam side down in greased baking pan. Cover with aluminum foil and heat in oven for 30 minutes. When ready to serve, arrange two crepes for each serving. Spoon Chicken Glaze over crepes. Makes 6 servings.

Chicken Glaze

- 4 tablespoons butter
- 4 tablespoons flour
- 3 cups chicken stock
- ½ teaspoon dried basil
- ½ teaspoon dried rosemary
- ½ teaspoon rubbed sage

Make a roux by melting butter in a heavy saucepan over medium-high heat until foamy. Stir in flour to make a golden, bubbly paste. Gradually add chicken stock and seasonings and cook until thickened, about 5 minutes.

Hearty Beef Stew

2   pounds beef chuck roast, cut in
        cubes
2   tablespoons vegetable oil
4   cups water
1   onion, sliced
1   clove garlic
1   tablespoon salt
1   tablespoon lemon juice
1   teaspoon sugar
1   teaspoon Worcestershire sauce
½   teaspoon black pepper
½   teaspoon paprika
2   bay leaves
    Dash ground allspice
6   carrots, cut in quarters
½   pound pearl onions
3   potatoes, peeled and cubed
¼   cup flour

Heat oil in heavy Dutch oven over medium-high heat; slowly brown beef cubes, turning often to brown meat on all sides. This should take about 15 minutes. Add water, onion slices, garlic clove (on toothpick so you can retrieve it later), salt, lemon juice, sugar, Worcestershire sauce, pepper, paprika, bay leaves, and allspice. Cover with lid and simmer on low heat (do not boil) for 2 hours. Stir occasionally to prevent sticking. When meat is almost done, add carrots, pearl onions, and potatoes, and simmer for 30 minutes more. Discard bay leaves and garlic. Pour ½ cup water in shaker and add ¼ cup flour; shake to blend. Either remove meat and vegetables from stock or move to one side in pan; stir in flour mixture. Cook and stir until gravy thickens and boils. Makes 8 servings.

Ginger Beef

2   pounds beef round steak
2   cloves garlic
        Dash of black pepper
1   10-ounce can beef broth
2   tablespoons cornstarch
¼   cup water
1   tablespoon soy sauce
¼   teaspoon crushed fresh ginger root
1   package frozen Chinese peapods
            or ¾ pound fresh peapods
2 to 3 cups hot cooked rice
        Cherry tomatoes, for garnishing

Trim fat from meat, then cut meat into thin strips. Coat a 12-inch skillet with nonstick cooking spray. Peel garlic and make several cuts on end of each clove; cook and stir in skillet over medium heat until browned. Remove and discard. In skillet in which garlic has been browned, cook meat over medium-high heat until browned, stirring occasionally. Sprinkle beef with pepper. Stir in broth and heat to boiling. Reduce heat and simmer uncovered until meat is tender, 10 to 15 minutes. (Add small amount of water if necessary.) Mix cornstarch, water, and soy sauce in a small bowl; stir into meat mixture. Cook, stirring constantly, until mixture thickens and boils. Boil and stir 1 minute. Stir in crushed gingerroot and peapods. Cook, stirring occasionally, until peapods are crisp-tender, about 5 minutes. Serve over rice. Garnish with cherry tomatoes. Makes 6 to 8 servings.

CABBAGE ROLLS

1 pound lean ground beef
1 cup ground ham
¼ cup chopped onion
⅓ cup tomato sauce
½ cup cooked rice
½ teaspoon chili powder
⅛ teaspoon garlic powder
2 medium heads cabbage
1 cup tomato sauce
¾ cup grated sharp cheddar cheese
½ teaspoon seasoned salt

Brown ground beef in a 12-inch skillet; drain off fat. Add ground ham, onion, ⅓ cup tomato sauce, rice, chili powder, and garlic powder; mix thoroughly. Core cabbage and remove 12 large outer leaves. Use remainder of cabbage for other recipes. Place leaves in boiling water in a medium saucepan and simmer for 5 minutes or until tender (leaves should be limp but not overcooked). Drain. Spoon meat mixture into center of each cabbage leaf. Fold up to make a tight roll and place seam-side down in a 9x13-inch baking pan. Mix 1 cup tomato sauce with grated cheese and seasoned salt. Pour over top of cabbage rolls. Or cover and refrigerate, then bake at 350 degrees for 30 minutes. Keep warm in oven set at 300 degrees until ready to serve. Makes 6 servings.

PARTY LASAGNA

1½ pounds ground beef
1½ tablespoons vegetable oil
1 clove garlic, minced
1 tablespoon parsley flakes
1 tablespoon dried basil
2 teaspoons salt
1 20-ounce can stewed tomatoes
1 6-ounce can tomato paste
1 10-ounce package lasagna noodles
3 cups large curd cottage cheese
2 eggs, beaten well
½ teaspoon pepper
2 tablespoons parsley flakes
½ cup grated Parmesan cheese
1 pound mozzarella cheese, thinly sliced

Preheat oven to 375 degrees. Brown ground beef in oil in a 12-inch skillet; drain off fat. Add garlic, 1 tablespoon parsley flakes, basil, and salt. Stir in tomatoes and tomato paste. Simmer uncovered until thick, about one hour, stirring occasionally.

Cook lasagna noodles as directed on package; drain and rinse in cold water. Mix cottage cheese with beaten eggs, pepper, 2 tablespoons parsley flakes, and Parmesan cheese. Place half of noodles in 9x13-inch baking pan. Spoon on half the cottage cheese mixture. Top cottage cheese with a layer of sliced mozzarella cheese, then spoon on a layer of meat mixture. Repeat layers, ending with layer of mozzarella on top. Bake 30 minutes. Makes 12 to 15 servings.

Stuffed Green Peppers

STUFFED GREEN PEPPERS

6   green bell peppers
1   pound ground beef
1   small onion
½   cup chopped celery
1   10.5-ounce can cream of mushroom
    soup
½   teaspoon dried oregano
½   teaspoon chili powder
½   teaspoon dried basil
½   teaspoon salt
1½ cups cooked rice
1   10.5-ounce can tomato soup
1   8-ounce can tomato sauce

Preheat oven to 350 degrees. Cut tops from green peppers; discard seeds. Cook peppers in small amount of boiling water for 5 minutes. Drain and arrange in a casserole dish; set aside. Brown ground beef and onion in a large skillet; drain off fat. Add celery, cream of mushroom soup, oregano, chili powder, basil, salt, and rice to ground beef. Mix well and spoon into green peppers. Combine tomato soup and tomato sauce in a small dish and pour over top of stuffed peppers. Bake 30 minutes. Makes 6 servings.

PORK TENDERLOIN

4   pork tenderloins (about 3 to 4
    pounds total)
3 to 4 cloves garlic, minced
½   cup soy sauce
½   cup sugar
¼ to ½ teaspoon ground ginger
    Red food coloring (optional)
    Chopped green onions and sesame
     seeds, for garnishing

Preheat oven to 325 degrees. Place tenderloins in large glass baking dish. Combine garlic, soy sauce, sugar, ginger, and a drop or two of red food coloring in a small bowl; pour over meat. Cover with plastic wrap and refrigerate for several hours or overnight, turning a couple of times. Remove plastic wrap and bake, covered with foil, for about 2 hours, or until meat thermometer registers 155 degrees. When ready to serve, slice at an angle into serving pieces. Place on serving platter and pour marinade on top. Garnish with chopped green onions and sesame seeds. Makes 6 to 8 servings.

Calico Beef and Bean Bake

Calico Beef and Bean Bake

½ to 1   pound ground beef
¾   pound bacon, cut in pieces
1   cup chopped onion
2   20-ounce cans pork and beans
1   16-ounce can dark red kidney beans, drained
1   16-ounce can butter beans
1   cup ketchup
¼   cup packed brown sugar
3   tablespoons white vinegar
1   teaspoon salt
   Black pepper to taste

Brown ground beef, bacon, and onion in a 12-inch skillet; drain off fat. Pour meat mixture into a baking dish or slow-cooker pot. Stir in remaining ingredients. Cook in baking dish in 325-degree oven for 1½ hours, or in an electric slow cooker set on low for 4 to 6 hours. Makes 8 servings.

Holiday Leg of Lamb

1   6- to 7-pound leg of lamb
2   cloves garlic, peeled and slivered
1   tablespoon vegetable oil
1   tablespoon fresh chopped rosemary
   Salt and pepper to taste
1   recipe Mint Sauce (see below)

Preheat oven to 375 degrees. Trim excess fat from lamb. With sharp paring knife, make small incisions all over the lamb. Insert a sliver of garlic into each incision. Rub lamb with oil and place in a roasting pan. Rub with rosemary, salt, and pepper. Roast for about 1½ hours, or until meat thermometer registers 145 degrees for medium rare or 165 degrees for well done. Serve with Mint Sauce. Makes 8 servings.

Mint Sauce

2   tablespoons sugar
½   cup white or cider vinegar
2   tablespoons water
½   cup minced fresh mint leaves

Prepare mint sauce by boiling sugar, vinegar, and water in a small saucepan. Pour over mint leaves and steep for 1 hour. Serve with sliced lamb roast.

LEMON-MARINATED SALMON

2	pounds salmon steaks or fillets
1	cup water
½	cup lemon juice
⅓	cup sliced green onion
¼	cup vegetable oil
3	tablespoons snipped parsley
3	tablespoons chopped green pepper
1	tablespoon sugar
2	teaspoons dry mustard
⅛	teaspoon cayenne pepper
½	teaspoon salt

Place fish on greased rack in a large skillet or fry pan. Pour in 1 cup water. Cover with a lid and steam for 5 to 7 minutes, or until fish is done and flakes easily when tested with a fork. Remove from pan to a shallow dish. Place the remaining ingredients in a screw-top jar and shake vigorously to combine; pour over fish. Cover and chill several hours or overnight, spooning marinade over fish several times. Drain before serving. Serve cold. Makes 6 servings.

HALIBUT BROIL AMANDINE

6	halibut steaks or fillets
1	cup chicken broth
2	tablespoons butter or margarine, melted
1	teaspoon dried thyme leaves
¼	cup butter or margarine
¼	cup sliced almonds
2	tablespoons lemon juice

Note: This cooking method works equally well for bass, cod, flounder, red snapper, shark, or orange roughy.

Preheat broiler in oven. Rinse fish and pat dry. Arrange in a single layer in a greased, broiler-safe baking pan. Pour broth around fish. Mix 2 tablespoons melted butter with thyme and brush half on fish. Place baking dish on broiler pan and place on oven rack about 3 to 4 inches from heat. Broil fish (do not turn), basting once or twice with remaining butter mixture. Broil 3 to 6 minutes for fish that is ½- to ¾-inch thick or 6 to 10 minutes for fish that is 1- to 1¼-inches thick. Melt ¼ cup butter in a small skillet. Add almonds and stir until nuts begin to brown. Remove from heat and add lemon juice. Pour over fish when ready to serve. Makes 6 servings.

Halibut Broil Amandine

ORANGE ROUGHY WITH DILL

2 tablespoons butter or margarine

1 pound orange roughy fish fillets, thawed

½ teaspoon dill weed

1 tablespoon lemon juice

Dash salt and pepper

Buttered bread crumbs*

Note: Any white-fleshed, mild-flavored fish, such as haddock, sole, or whitefish, may be substituted for the orange roughy.

Preheat oven to 450 degrees. Melt butter in shallow baking dish in oven while oven is preheating. Remove dish from oven and place fish in melted butter, turning to coat; sprinkle with dill weed, lemon juice, and salt and pepper. Bake for 15 to 20 minutes, or until fish flakes easily with fork. Sprinkle lightly with buttered bread crumbs during last 3 minutes of baking. Makes 4 servings.

* To make buttered bread crumbs, melt 1 tablespoon butter and mix with 1 cup bread crumbs until crumbs are coated.

CRAB TETRAZZINI

8 ounces dry spaghetti, broken in pieces 3 to 4 inches long

2 10.5-ounce cans cream of mushroom soup

1½ cups milk

5 tablespoons butter

¼ cup chopped green pepper

1 cup grated cheddar cheese

½ cup grated Parmesan cheese

1 pound imitation crabmeat

Preheat oven to 350 degrees. Cook broken spaghetti pieces in boiling salted water according to package directions; drain and set aside. Mix soup, milk, butter, and green pepper together in a large saucepan and warm over medium heat until butter is melted. Mix well. Add cooked spaghetti, cheddar cheese, Parmesan cheese, and imitation crabmeat. Pour into a 9x13-inch baking dish or large casserole dish. Cover and bake until bubbly, 30 to 40 minutes. If desired, sprinkle additional grated cheese on top of casserole near the end of baking time. Makes 10 to 12 servings.

HOLIDAY OVEN OMELET

¼ cup butter or margarine

9 large eggs

1 cup sour cream

1 cup milk

2 teaspoons salt

¼ cup chopped chives or green onion

1 recipe English Sausage Rolls (see below)

Preheat oven to 325 degrees. Melt butter or margarine in 9x13-inch baking dish while oven is preheating. In a large bowl beat eggs, then add sour cream, milk, salt, and chopped chives. Mix well. Pour into dish with melted butter. Bake for 35 minutes or until eggs are done but still moist. Serve with English Sausage Rolls. Makes 8 to 10 servings.

ENGLISH SAUSAGE ROLLS

2 pounds bulk sausage

2 cups flour

½ teaspoon salt

4 teaspoons baking powder

1 tablespoon sugar

⅓ cup shortening

1 egg, beaten well

½ cup milk

Note: This recipe uses shortcake dough to wrap up the sausages, but pie dough will work as well.

Preheat oven to 400 degrees. Form sausage into 12 patties and brown lightly in a large skillet. (Brown patties in batches to get even browning.) Drain off fat and pat patties with paper towel to remove grease. Sift flour, salt, baking powder, and sugar into a large mixing bowl; cut in shortening with a pastry blender or fork until mixture resembles coarse crumbs. Add egg and milk and stir just enough to moisten. Roll out on slightly floured board. Cut squares of dough and wrap around each sausage patty. Place on greased baking sheet and bake for 15 minutes, or until pastry is golden brown. Serve with ketchup or chili sauce. Makes 12 sausage rolls.

MEXICAN QUICHE

½ pound ground pork sausage

½ cup sliced green onion

2 cloves garlic, minced

1 4-ounce can diced green chili
   peppers, drained

2 cups (8 ounces) grated American
   or cheddar cheese

2 tablespoons flour

1 cup light cream or milk

½ teaspoon hot pepper sauce

4 eggs, beaten well

1 9-inch pastry shell, baked for 10
   minutes in a 375-degree oven

Note: Instead of using a traditional pie crust, you can shape one 8-ounce can of Pillsbury® Refrigerated Crescent Dinner Rolls into a pie shell in the bottom of a 9-inch pie plate.

Preheat oven to 325 degrees. In a 12-inch skillet, brown sausage, onions, and garlic over medium-high heat; drain off fat. Stir in chilies and set aside. Toss cheese and flour in a medium saucepan; pour in cream and cook and stir over medium heat until cheese is melted. Add hot pepper sauce. Gradually blend beaten eggs into hot cream mixture. Stir in meat mixture and pour into pastry shell. Bake 20 to 25 minutes, or until knife inserted 2 inches from pastry's edge comes out clean. Let stand 10 minutes before serving. Makes 6 to 8 servings.

BAKED FRENCH TOAST

1 loaf French bread, cut diagonally
   in 1-inch slices

6 eggs

2 cups milk

1½ cups half-and-half

2 teaspoons vanilla extract

1 teaspoon ground cinnamon

¾ cup butter

1⅓ cups packed brown sugar

3 tablespoons light corn syrup

Note: Prepare this recipe on Christmas Eve, pop it in the oven first thing Christmas morning, and enjoy a delicious, no-hassle breakfast.

Coat a 9x13-inch baking dish with nonstick cooking spray. Arrange bread slices in the bottom of the pan; set aside. In a large bowl, beat together eggs, milk, half-and-half, vanilla, and cinnamon. Pour over bread slices, cover, and refrigerate overnight. The next morning, preheat oven to 350 degrees. In a small saucepan, combine butter, brown sugar, and corn syrup. Heat until bubbling. Pour over bread and egg mixture. Bake uncovered for 40 minutes. Serve with butter, syrup, and powdered sugar. Makes 8 to 10 servings.

Baked Apple French Toast with Caramel Sauce

1   loaf French bread, sliced in 1½-inch slices
6   eggs
1½   cups milk
½   cup sugar
1   tablespoon vanilla
6   medium apples, peeled and sliced (Fuji, Jonathan, or Granny Smith)
1½   teaspoons ground cinnamon
½   teaspoon ground nutmeg
3   tablespoons packed brown sugar
1   recipe Caramel Sauce (see below)

The night before serving, coat a 9x13-inch baking dish with nonstick cooking spray. Layer bread slices on the bottom of the pan. Combine eggs, milk, sugar, and vanilla in a large bowl; beat well and pour over bread slices. Place apple slices on top of bread. Sprinkle apples with cinnamon, nutmeg, and brown sugar. Cover with foil and refrigerate overnight. In the morning, preheat oven to 350 degrees. Bake covered about 50 minutes; remove foil and bake 10 minutes more. Serve toast hot, topped with Caramel Sauce. Makes 8 to 10 servings.

Caramel Sauce

½   cup packed brown sugar
¼   cup flour
½   cup butter, melted
½   cup milk
2   teaspoons vanilla

Combine all ingredients in a medium saucepan and cook over medium heat until thick, stirring constantly.

Zucchini Boats

ZUCCHINI BOATS

3   medium zucchini squash
1½   cups soft bread crumbs
¼   cup grated Parmesan cheese
1   egg, beaten well
2   green onions, minced
1   tablespoon minced parsley
½   teaspoon salt
       Paprika
       Grated Parmesan cheese

Preheat oven to 350 degrees. Wash zucchini; cut off ends but don't peel. Cook in boiling, salted water for 7 to 10 minutes. Drain off water and cut zucchini in half lengthwise; carefully remove pulp with spoon, leaving shell intact. In a small bowl mash zucchini pulp with fork and mix with bread crumbs, Parmesan cheese, beaten egg, onions, parsley, and salt. Spoon mixture into zucchini shells and place in baking dish. Sprinkle with additional Parmesan cheese and paprika. Bake, uncovered, for 30 minutes. Makes 6 servings.

FESTIVE BEETS

1   16-ounce can diced beets
¼   cup sour cream
1   tablespoon tarragon or cider
          vinegar
1   teaspoon sugar
½   teaspoon salt
1   green onion, minced
       Dash cayenne pepper

Warm beets in a small saucepan over medium heat; drain off liquid. Stir in sour cream, tarragon or cider vinegar, sugar, salt, onion, and cayenne pepper. Continue to heat slowly over medium heat. When hot, serve immediately. Makes 4 servings.

CARROTS LYONNAISE

1 chicken bouillon cube
½ cup boiling water
6 medium carrots, peeled and julienned
2 tablespoons butter
2 medium onions, sliced
1 tablespoon flour
¼ teaspoon salt
 Dash pepper
 Pinch sugar
¾ cup water

Dissolve bouillon cube in boiling water in a medium saucepan. Add carrots; return to boiling, then reduce heat to a simmer and cook for 7 to 10 minutes, until crisp-tender. While carrots are cooking, melt butter in a small skillet over medium-high heat. Add sliced onions and sauté until translucent. Add flour, salt, pepper, sugar, and ¾ cup water. Stir until thickened. Stir in cooked carrots and the cooking water. Stir until all ingredients are blended. Serve hot. Makes 6 servings.

ROASTED ROOT VEGETABLES

1 large onion
2 large carrots
1 large potato
2 large parsnips
2 large turnips
3 tablespoons canola oil
1 teaspoon cracked black pepper
1 teaspoon kosher salt
1 red bell pepper
1 green bell pepper
1 tablespoon chopped fresh parsley

Preheat oven to 375 degrees. Thoroughly clean all vegetables. Peel onion and carrots. Slice or chop all vegetables into bite-sized pieces, keeping each separate. Combine hard root vegetables (carrots, potatoes, parsnips, and turnips) in a large mixing bowl. Add 2 tablespoons oil and ½ teaspoon pepper and ½ teaspoon salt. Toss well until vegetables are evenly coated. Spread vegetables out evenly in one layer in a large baking pan and place in oven. Toss remaining vegetables in remaining oil, pepper, and salt. When vegetables in oven are slightly tender, remove from oven and add remaining vegetables to pan. Return to oven and continue roasting until all vegetables are tender and begin to brown. Serve hot, garnished with chopped fresh parsley.

* Any combination of vegetables will work well. Use whatever you like. Other vegetables recommended are zucchini, yellow squash, any hard winter squash, or beets. Beets will tend to color the other vegetables, so keep them separate until served. Remember to add softer vegetables later to avoid overcooking. Makes 6 to 8 servings.

3 o

Roasted Root Vegetables

Snow-Whipped Potato Boats

Snow-Whipped Potato Boats

6   large baking potatoes
3   slices bacon, cooked crisp and crumbled
½   cup sour cream
½   cup milk
1   teaspoon salt
⅛   teaspoon pepper
4   green onions, chopped
½   cup grated cheddar cheese

Preheat oven to 400 degrees. Wash potatoes and rub skins with vegetable oil. Bake for 1 hour, or until potatoes are fork-tender. Remove potatoes from oven and reduce oven heat to 350 degrees. Cut a slice from top of each potato and scoop out pulp. In a medium bowl mash pulp with a fork, then stir in sour cream, milk, salt, pepper, and green onions. Whip until fluffy. Fill potato shells with mixture and sprinkle with grated cheese and crumbled bacon. Bake 10 minutes. Makes 6 servings.

Nutmeg Spinach Soufflé

1   pound fresh spinach
2   tablespoons margarine
2   tablespoons flour
1   teaspoon salt
1   cup milk
4   egg yolks, beaten well
¼   cup chopped onion
⅛   teaspoon ground nutmeg
4   egg whites
¼   teaspoon cream of tartar
3   tablespoons grated Parmesan cheese

Preheat oven to 375 degrees. Wash spinach; cook in small amount of salted water in a medium saucepan until tender. Drain; press out all excess water with paper towels or a clean dish towel. Chop spinach and set aside.

Make a roux by melting margarine in a heavy saucepan over medium-high heat. When margarine is melted and foamy, stir in flour and salt. Cook and stir until golden and fragrant, about 30 seconds to 1 minute. Gradually add milk, cooking and stirring until thickened. Gradually add beaten egg yolks. Stir in spinach, onion, and nutmeg. Remove from heat.

In a large clean bowl, beat egg whites and cream of tartar until stiff peaks form. Fold in spinach mixture. Pour into a greased soufflé dish or 1½ quart casserole dish. Sprinkle with Parmesan cheese. Bake for 50 minutes or until table knife inserted in center comes out clean. Makes 6 servings.

LEMON-PARSLEY TURNIPS

3   medium turnips
1   tablespoon butter
2   teaspoons freshly snipped parsley
1   teaspoon finely chopped green onion
1   teaspoon lemon juice

Peel and cut turnips into 2-inch strips, julienne style. Cook in small amount of boiling, salted water, until tender, about 10 minutes. Drain off water. Toss parsnips in a medium bowl with butter, parsley, onion, and lemon juice. Makes 6 servings.

CROOKNECK SQUASH SCALLOP

3   medium yellow crookneck squash
1/2   teaspoon salt
1   cup water
1   medium onion, sliced
1/4   cup margarine
1/4   cup flour
2 1/2 cups milk
1   teaspoon salt
2   tablespoons chopped pimientos
1   cup cracker crumbs (Ritz®, for
          example)
3   tablespoons margarine, melted

Preheat oven to 350 degrees. Wash and slice squash. Place squash, 1/2 teaspoon salt, and water in a medium saucepan and bring to a boil. Cook for 8 to 10 minutes. Add sliced onions and continue cooking for another 5 minutes. Drain vegetables and remove to a casserole dish. Make a white sauce by melting margarine over medium-high heat in a heavy saucepan. Stir in flour to make a roux and cook and stir until bubbly and golden, about 30 seconds to 1 minute. Slowly add milk and stir over medium heat until thickened. Stir in 1 teaspoon salt and chopped pimientos. Pour sauce over squash. Combine cracker crumbs and melted margarine in a small bowl. Sprinkle on top of casserole. Bake 20 minutes. Makes 6 servings.

ITALIAN ZUCCHINI BAKE

2 tablespoons vegetable oil

1½ pounds zucchini, cut into ¼-inch cubes (about 5 cups)

1 cup sliced green onion

1 clove garlic, pressed

1½ cups stewed tomatoes

1 teaspoon garlic salt

½ teaspoon dried basil

½ teaspoon dried oregano leaves

½ teaspoon paprika

1 cup cooked rice

2 cups grated sharp cheddar cheese

Preheat oven to 350 degrees. Heat oil in a 12-inch skillet over medium heat. Stir in zucchini, onions, and garlic; cover and cook for 5 minutes. Remove from heat and mix in tomatoes, garlic salt, basil, oregano, paprika, rice, and 1 cup cheese. Spoon mixture into a shallow 1½-quart baking dish and sprinkle with remaining 1 cup cheese. Bake, uncovered, for 25 minutes. Makes 6 servings.

ITALIAN ZUCCHINI CRESCENT PIE

½ cup butter or margarine

1 cup chopped onion

4 cups thinly sliced unpeeled zucchini

2 eggs, beaten well

2 cups (8 ounces) grated Muenster or mozzarella cheese

½ cup fresh chopped parsley or 2 tablespoons parsley flakes

½ teaspoon salt

½ teaspoon ground black pepper

1 clove garlic, crushed, or ¼ teaspoon garlic powder

1 teaspoon freshly chopped basil, or ¼ teaspoon dried basil

¼ teaspoon dried oregano

2 teaspoons prepared mustard

1 8-ounce can Pillsbury® Refrigerated Crescent Dinner Rolls

Note: You can easily turn this recipe into an appetizer by using 2 cans refrigerated rolls. Place a little bit of filling on each crescent and roll up. Place on cookie sheets and bake according to package directions.

Preheat oven to 375 degrees. Melt butter in a large skillet over medium-high heat. Add onion and zucchini and sauté until tender; remove from heat and set aside. Combine beaten eggs, cheese, parsley, salt, pepper, garlic, basil, oregano, and mustard in a large bowl. Stir in zucchini mixture and mix well. Use crescent rolls to make a pie crust in a 10-inch pie plate. Pour filling into crust. Bake 18 to 20 minutes. Top of pie will be slightly golden. Makes 6 servings.

Challah Braid

CHALLAH BRAID

1 tablespoon dry yeast
1½ cups water (110 to 115 degrees)
¼ cup sugar
¼ cup vegetable oil
1 teaspoon salt
2 eggs, beaten well
Pinch of saffron (optional)
4½ to 5 cups flour
1 egg yolk, beaten well
¼ teaspoon water
Sesame seeds

Place yeast and water in a large bowl. Stir slightly to dissolve. Add sugar, oil, salt, beaten eggs, saffron, and 2½ cups flour. Beat well. Add enough remaining flour to make a soft dough; knead until smooth. Place in a greased bowl. Cover and let rise until double in bulk (30 to 40 minutes). Punch down dough and divide into 6 pieces. Roll each piece into a long rope, 18 to 20 inches long and 1 inch in diameter. Braid three of the ropes together. Repeat with the remaining 3 pieces of dough. Place on greased cookie sheet. Mix egg yolk with ¼ teaspoon water and brush over braids. Sprinkle with sesame seeds. Cover and let rise 30 minutes. Bake at 375 degrees about 30 to 35 minutes. Makes 2 braids.

POTATO WHEAT BREAD

1 medium potato
2 cups potato water
1 tablespoon dry yeast
¼ cup warm water (110 to 115 degrees)
2 tablespoons honey
2 teaspoons salt
2 tablespoons vegetable oil
3 cups whole wheat flour
3 cups white flour

Peel and dice one medium potato. Place in a medium saucepan and cover with about 3 cups water. Bring to a boil, then simmer until tender. Drain, saving 2 cups potato water; set aside. Mash potato and set aside.

Dissolve yeast in ¼ cup warm water in a large bowl. Add potato water, mashed potato, honey, salt, oil, and 2 cups whole wheat flour. Beat together for 5 minutes on low speed. Continue adding wheat and white flour until dough can be handled for kneading. Turn onto lightly floured surface and knead into a smooth ball, about 5 minutes. Place in a greased bowl; cover and let rise until double in bulk (40 to 50 minutes). Punch down and knead again, about 5 minutes. Cover and let rise again (30 minutes). Divide dough in half, and shape into loaves. Brush the sides and bottom of 2 loaf pans (approximately 4½ x 8-inch) with vegetable oil or spray with non-stick vegetable spray. Allow loaves to rise 30 minutes. Bake at 375 degrees for 30 to 35 minutes. Makes 2 loaves.

PINWHEEL BREAD

3   cups warm water (110 to 115 degrees)

2   tablespoons dry yeast

1/3 cup honey

1/3 cup vegetable oil

1   tablespoon salt

1   cup powdered milk

7   cups all-purpose flour (substitute 7 cups whole wheat flour to make whole wheat dough)

Note: This recipe uses both white and whole-wheat dough. Prepare the white dough first, then repeat the ingredients list and directions below to prepare whole wheat dough.

Prepare the white dough: Pour warm water into a large mixing bowl. Add yeast, honey, oil, salt, and milk. Stir in 3 cups flour and beat well. Add remaining flour, 1 cup at a time, until soft dough is formed. Knead on a lightly floured board until smooth and elastic, about 7 to 10 minutes. Place in a greased bowl; cover and let rise until double in bulk (45 to 60 minutes). While white dough is rising, prepare the whole wheat dough as described in note above.

Punch down dough. Divide each batch of dough into 6 equal portions. Roll 1 portion of white dough into a rectangle, then roll 1 portion of the wheat dough into a rectangle and place on top of white rectangle. Roll up like a jelly roll, sealing ends and bottom. Place in greased 4½ x 8-inch loaf pan. Let rise in warm place until doubled in bulk (30 to 40 minutes). Bake at 350 degrees for 35 minutes. Makes 6 loaves.

GRANARY BREAD

1½ tablespoons dry yeast

3½ cups warm water (110 to 115 degrees)

1/2 cup vegetable oil

1/2 cup honey

1/4 cup molasses

1   tablespoon salt

1½ cups quick-cooking oats

1½ cups cracked wheat

1/2 cup wheat germ

1/2 cup soy flour

4½ cups whole wheat flour

2   cups white flour

Dissolve yeast in warm water in a large mixing bowl. Add oil, honey, molasses, salt, oats, cracked wheat, wheat germ, and soy flour. Beat well. Gradually add whole wheat and white flours to form a stiff dough. Turn onto a lightly floured surface and knead until smooth and elastic, 5 to 7 minutes. Place in a greased bowl; cover and let rise until double in bulk (30 to 40 minutes). Punch down, divide dough into thirds, and mold into loaves. Place in greased 4½ x 8-inch loaf pans. Let rise until doubled (30 minutes). Bake at 350 degrees for 30 minutes. Makes 3 loaves.

CRUNCHY ONION LOAF

1   tablespoon dry yeast
¼   cup warm water (110 to 115
          degrees)
1   envelope dry onion soup mix
2   cups water
2   tablespoons sugar
1   teaspoon salt
2   tablespoons grated Parmesan cheese
2   tablespoons shortening
1   egg yolk, beaten well
5 to 5½ cups flour
          Cornmeal
1   egg white, beaten well

Soften yeast in ¼ cup water in a small bowl; set aside. Combine soup mix and 2 cups water in saucepan and simmer 10 minutes. Add sugar, salt, Parmesan cheese, and shortening. Cool to lukewarm. Pour in a large bowl and add egg yolk, softened yeast, and 2 cups flour. Beat 3 minutes. Add 1½ cups flour and beat until well mixed. Place 1 cup flour on cupboard, turn dough out on it and knead until smooth and elastic (5 to 7 minutes). If dough is sticky, add ½ cup flour and continue to knead until smooth. Place in greased or oiled bowl, cover and let rise until double in bulk (40 to 50 minutes). Punch down and divide in half. Shape into two round loaves. Place on greased baking sheet sprinkled with cornmeal. Cut several diagonal slashes on top of loaf and brush with slightly beaten egg white. Bake at 375 degrees for 30 minutes. Makes 2 rounds.

CRUSTY SOUP BOWLS

2   tablespoons dry yeast
2   cups warm water (110 to 115
          degrees)
1   tablespoon sugar
2   teaspoons salt
5   cups flour
          Cornmeal
1   egg
1   tablespoon water

Dissolve yeast in 2 cups warm water in a large mixing bowl. Add sugar, salt, and 3 cups flour; beat 3 minutes on low speed. Gradually add enough remaining flour to make a stiff dough. Knead on a lightly floured surface until dough is smooth and elastic, 5 to 6 minutes. Place in a greased bowl, cover and let rise until doubled, about 40 minutes. Punch down, and divide into 8 pieces. Form each piece into a ball and place on a baking sheet sprinkled with cornmeal. Beat egg and water together and brush over top and sides of dough balls. Cover and let rise until double in bulk, about 40 minutes. Bake at 375 degrees for 25 minutes. Cool. Cut off tops; scoop out bread to make a bowl. Pour hot soup into bread bowl and serve. Makes 8 large bread bowls.

HOLIDAY ALMOND TWISTS

1 tablespoon dry yeast

½ cup warm water (110 to 115 degrees)

4½ cups flour

¼ cup sugar

1 teaspoon salt

1 teaspoon orange zest

1 cup butter, softened

6 eggs

1 recipe Holiday Almond Twist Filling (see below)

1 recipe Pastry Glaze (see below)

Dissolve yeast in warm water in a large mixing bowl. Add 3 cups flour, sugar, salt, orange zest, butter, and eggs. Beat on low speed of electric mixer until blended. Increase speed to medium and beat 4 minutes. Add remaining flour and continue beating at low speed until flour is incorporated. Cover dough and let rise in a warm place until doubled in size, about 40 to 50 minutes. Punch down; cover and refrigerate at least 8 hours.

Several hours before serving, remove dough from fridge and punch down; divide in half. Place first half on a lightly floured surface and roll to a 10x16-inch rectangle. Spread the dough with half of the Almond Filling. Fold the dough lengthwise into thirds, forming a long rectangle. Cut rectangle into 16 1-inch strips. Twist each strip and place on greased baking sheet. Repeat with remaining dough and filling. Cover and let rise in a warm place until doubled, about 20 minutes. Bake at 350 degrees for 15 minutes or until golden brown. Remove from oven. Drizzle Pastry Glaze over warm rolls. Makes 32 twists.

Holiday Almond Twist Filling

1 8-ounce can almond paste

½ cup butter, softened

¾ cup packed brown sugar

¼ cup chopped almonds, toasted*

Combine almond paste, butter, brown sugar, and chopped toasted almonds in a small bowl and blend well.

*To toast almonds, spread on a baking sheet and toast in a 350-degree oven for 5 to 8 minutes, until golden brown and fragrant.

Pastry Glaze

2 cups sifted powdered sugar

3 tablespoons milk

Combine well and drizzle over warm rolls.

YULETIDE DANISH PASTRY

1/2 cup warm water (110 to 115 degrees)
2 cups warm milk
2 tablespoons dry yeast
1 cup butter or margarine, softened
3/4 cup sugar, plus 1 tablespoon
1 teaspoon salt
2 eggs
8 cups flour
1 recipe Cream Filling (see below)
1 recipe Almond Filling (see below)
1 recipe Streusel Topping (see below)
1 recipe Almond Icing (see below)
Slivered or sliced almonds, for garnishing

In a large bowl, place water and warm milk. Sprinkle yeast over the mixture and then sprinkle sugar over the yeast. Add softened butter, salt, eggs, and 2 cups flour. Beat for about 2 minutes with mixer. Add 2 more cups flour and beat again with mixer for 2 minutes. Add remaining flour and knead until smooth, about 5 minutes. Cover and let rise until double, about 45 minutes. Punch down. Divide dough into 4 equal parts. On lightly floured board, roll each part into a rectangle. Spread 1/4 Cream Filling on each; then 1/4 Almond Filling on each. Roll up jelly-roll fashion. Cut about 10 slashes through top of rolls with a serrated knife. Place each roll on a greased cookie sheet, then form into a wreath shape or candy cane shape. Sprinkle with Streusel Topping. Let rise in a warm place until double in bulk, about 30 minutes. Bake at 375 degrees for 20 minutes. Drizzle warm bread with Almond Icing and sprinkle with slivered or sliced almonds.

Cream Filling

1 cup milk
1/2 teaspoon salt
1/3 cup sugar
2 tablespoons flour
1 egg yolk

Heat milk in a small saucepan over medium heat. In a separate bowl, combine dry ingredients, then mix in egg yolk. Stir a tablespoon or two of warmed milk into egg mixture, then add egg mixture to the heated milk. Cook and stir over medium-high heat until mixture is bubbly and thick. Cover tightly with plastic wrap and cool.

Almond Filling

1/2 cup butter or margarine
3/4 cup sugar
1/2 cup oats
2 teaspoons almond flavoring

Combine all ingredients with a fork, wire whisk, or electric mixer until well blended.

Streusel Topping

1/2 cup flour
1/2 cup sugar
1/2 cup butter

Mix all ingredients with a fork, wire whisk, or electric mixer until well blended.

Almond Icing

1 cup powdered sugar
2 to 3 tablespoons milk or cream
1 teaspoon almond flavoring

Combine powdered sugar with enough milk or cream to make a slightly runny icing. Stir in almond flavoring.

English Wigs

ENGLISH WIGS

2 tablespoons dry yeast
1/2 cup warm water (110 to 115 degrees)
1/2 cup sugar
1/2 cup margarine, melted
1 3/4 cups warm milk
1 egg, beaten well
2 teaspoons salt
1 1/2 teaspoons ground nutmeg
1/8 teaspoon ground cloves
1/8 teaspoon mace
5 1/2 to 6 1/2 cups flour
1 egg, for egg wash
Caraway seeds

Note: Serve these caraway-topped buns with hot spiced cider on Christmas Eve, or with raspberry jam as a Christmas-morning breakfast treat.

Dissolve yeast in warm water in a large mixing bowl. Stir in sugar, melted margarine, milk, beaten egg, salt, nutmeg, cloves, and mace. Add 3 cups flour and beat with electric mixer on low speed until smooth. Gradually add enough additional flour to make a soft dough. Turn out onto a lightly floured surface and knead until smooth and elastic, about 5 to 6 minutes. Place in greased bowl; cover and let rise until dough doubles in bulk, about 45 minutes. Punch down. Divide dough in half. Form 12 round buns and place on greased baking sheet. Repeat with other half of dough. Cut a deep cross on each bun with a sharp knife. Make an egg wash by beating an egg; brush over each bun. Sprinkle tops with caraway seeds. Cover and let rise until doubled, about 45 minutes. Bake at 375 degrees for 20 minutes. Makes 24 buns.

CARAMEL-NUT BOW KNOTS

1/2 recipe Potato Wheat Bread dough (see page 79)
1 cup packed brown sugar
1/2 cup light corn syrup
4 tablespoons butter
1 1/2 teaspoons water
3/4 cup chopped nuts
1/2 cup sugar
1 tablespoon ground cinnamon

Prepare dough for Potato Wheat Bread through the second rise time; set aside. Mix brown sugar, corn syrup, butter, and water in a medium saucepan. Heat over medium heat until butter is melted; simmer 3 to 4 minutes until it looks like syrup. Spread in bottom of a 9x13-inch baking dish. Sprinkle chopped nuts on top of syrup mixture.

Combine 1/2 cup sugar and cinnamon together in a shallow dish. Pinch off a small amount of Potato Wheat Bread dough and roll between your hands to make a 6-inch rope. Tie rope in a knot. Dip the knot into the sugar-cinnamon mixture and place on top of syrup in pan. Repeat until pan is full of bow knots. Place pan in a warm place to rise until doubled in bulk, about 40 minutes. Bake at 350 degrees for 20 to 25 minutes. Remove from oven and immediately turn over onto waxed paper to let syrup drip down through the bow knots. Makes 12 medium rolls.

ORANGE ROLLS

1   recipe dough for Lion House Dinner
      Rolls (see page 84)
½   cup butter, melted
      Zest from two oranges
¼   cup sugar
1   recipe Orange Icing (see below)

After dough for Lion House Dinner Rolls has risen the first time, roll dough to rectangle about ¼-inch thick. Combine melted butter and orange zest in a small bowl; brush over dough. Sprinkle with sugar. With pizza cutter or very sharp knife, cut dough in half to make two strips about 4 inches wide. Make cuts through strips of dough every 2 inches, making about 18 pieces of dough. Roll up strips, starting with narrow edge. Place on lightly greased baking sheet. Allow to rise until double in size, about 40 minutes. Bake at 375 degrees for 12 to 15 minutes, until light golden brown. Remove from oven and brush with melted butter. Allow to cool about 10 to 15 minutes; drizzle with Orange Icing. Makes 18 rolls.

Orange Icing

1½   cups powdered sugar
2   tablespoons freshly squeezed orange
       juice (reserve from zested oranges
       used in Orange Rolls recipe
       above)
2 to 4   tablespoons heavy cream, or
         2 tablespoons half-and-half

Note: You can add more orange flavor by mixing in 1 to 2 teaspoons orange zest if desired.

Place powdered sugar and orange juice in a small bowl; add half the amount of heavy cream. With spoon or mixer, mix until smooth. If icing is too thick, add more cream a little at a time. The hotter the rolls are when frosted, the thicker the frosting needs to be.

REFRIGERATOR ROLLS

1   cup shortening, melted
½   cup sugar
4   eggs
2½   cups water
2   tablespoons dry yeast
2   teaspoons salt
7   cups flour

Note: You can use this recipe to make wheat rolls as well. Use 4 cups whole wheat flour and 3 cups white flour.

Mix melted shortening, sugar, eggs, water, yeast, and salt with 3 cups flour in a 5-quart bowl. Gradually add rest of flour, 1 cup at a time, beating on low speed to make a soft dough. Cover tightly and refrigerate overnight. Two to three hours before baking, remove from refrigerator. Roll out on lightly floured surface. For Parkerhouse rolls, cut with biscuit cutter in circles; fold in half and place on greased cookie sheets. Allow to rise until double in bulk, about 45 minutes. Bake at 375 degrees for 15 minutes. Makes 4 dozen rolls.

LEMON-GLAZED POPPY SEED BREAD

1¼ cups milk
⅓ cup vegetable oil
1 egg
1 teaspoon vanilla
1 teaspoon rum flavoring (optional)
2½ cups flour
1 cup sugar
¼ cup poppy seeds
3 teaspoons baking powder
1 teaspoon salt
½ cup powdered sugar
1 tablespoon lemon juice

Preheat oven to 350 degrees. Grease bottoms only of 1 large (4½x8-inch) loaf pan or 2 small (2½ x 4-inch) loaf pans. In a small bowl combine milk, oil, egg, vanilla, and rum flavoring. In a separate mixing bowl, combine flour, sugar, poppy seeds, baking powder, and salt. Add liquid ingredients to dry ingredients and stir 30 seconds. Pour batter into pan(s). Bake for 50 to 60 minutes (25 to 30 minutes for small loaf pans). Loosen sides of loaf from pan with a sharp knife; remove from pan. Combine powdered sugar and lemon juice in a small bowl and drizzle over bread while still warm. Cool completely before slicing. Makes 1 large loaf or 2 small loaves.

Wholesome Breads

Light Fruit Cake, Lion House Pumpkin Bread, Lemon-Glazed Poppy Seed Bread, Cranberry Nut Loaf

CRANBERRY NUT LOAF

2 cups flour
³/₄ cup sugar
1 teaspoon baking powder
½ teaspoon baking soda
1 teaspoon salt
⅓ cup butter
2 eggs, beaten well
³/₄ cup orange juice
1 tablespoon orange zest
1 cup chopped fresh cranberries
½ cup chopped nuts

Preheat oven to 350 degrees. Combine flour, sugar, baking powder, baking soda, and salt in a large mixing bowl. Add butter, eggs, orange juice, and orange zest and stir just to moisten. Fold in cranberries and nuts. Grease bottom only of 1 large (4½ x 8-inch) loaf pan or 2 small (2½ x 4-inch) loaf pans. Pour batter into pan(s). Bake 50 to 60 minutes (25 to 30 minutes for small loaf pans). Cool slightly; loosen sides of loaf from pan with a sharp knife and remove. Cool completely before slicing. Makes 1 large or 2 small loaves.

LION HOUSE PUMPKIN BREAD

1⅓ cups vegetable oil
5 eggs
1 16-ounce can pumpkin
2 cups flour
2 cups sugar
1 teaspoon salt
1 teaspoon ground cinnamon
1 teaspoon ground nutmeg
1 teaspoon baking soda
2 3-ounce packages instant vanilla
    pudding mix
1 cup chopped nuts

Preheat oven to 350 degrees. Combine oil, eggs, and pumpkin in a large mixing bowl and beat well. In a separate bowl sift together flour, sugar, salt, cinnamon, nutmeg, and baking soda. Add to pumpkin mixture and mix until blended. Stir in pudding mix and nuts. Pour into a greased 4½ x 8-inch loaf pans. Bake for 1 hour. Makes 2 loaves.

WHOLE WHEAT MUFFINS

1 cup whole wheat flour
1 cup white flour
½ cup packed brown sugar
½ teaspoon salt
4 teaspoons baking powder
⅓ cup shortening, melted
2 eggs, beaten well
1 cup milk
1 cup chopped walnuts

Preheat oven to 375 degrees. Grease a 12-cup muffin tin or line with muffin papers. Combine flours, brown sugar, salt, and baking powder in a medium mixing bowl. Make a well in the mixture and add melted shortening, eggs, and milk. Mix until just moistened. Fold in chopped nuts. Spoon into muffin cups, filling three-fourths full. Bake for 20 to 25 minutes. Makes 12 muffins.

OATMEAL APPLE MUFFINS

1 cup flour

3 teaspoons baking powder

⅓ cup packed brown sugar

1 cup quick-cooking oats

2 teaspoons ground cinnamon

1 teaspoon ground nutmeg

½ teaspoon salt

1 egg, beaten well

¾ cup milk

½ cup vegetable oil

1 cup raisins

1 apple, peeled, cored, and chopped

Preheat oven to 400 degrees. Grease a 12-cup muffin tin or line with muffin papers. Mix together with a spoon the flour, baking powder, brown sugar, oats, cinnamon, nutmeg, and salt in a large bowl. In a separate bowl, combine beaten egg, milk, vegetable oil, raisins, and chopped apple. Fold wet ingredients into dry ingredients, mixing just to moisten. Spoon batter into greased muffin cups, filling three-fourths full. Bake for 15 to 20 minutes until lightly golden and a toothpick inserted in the middle of one muffin comes out clean. Makes 12 muffins.

GOLD-RUSH MUFFINS

3 eggs (or 6 egg whites)

⅓ cup packed brown sugar

½ cup vegetable oil

¼ cup molasses

2 cups unprocessed wheat bran

1 cup grated carrots

1 cup mashed bananas (2 large bananas)

1½ cups apple juice or milk

1½ cups whole wheat flour

½ cup untoasted wheat germ

1 teaspoon baking soda

2 teaspoons baking powder

1 teaspoon salt

2 teaspoons ground cinnamon

½ cup raisins

Preheat oven to 375 degrees. Grease a 12-cup muffin tin or line with muffin papers. Beat eggs in a large bowl. Add brown sugar, oil, molasses, bran, carrots, bananas, and apple juice or milk. Stir well; set aside. In a separate bowl, combine whole wheat flour, wheat germ, baking soda, baking powder, salt, and cinnamon; stir in raisins, then add all at once to egg mixture, stirring only until moistened. Spoon into muffin cups, filling three-fourths full. Bake for 25 minutes. Makes 2 dozen muffins.

CURRANT-CREAM SCONES

1¾   cups flour
3   tablespoons sugar
2½   teaspoons baking powder
½   teaspoon salt
⅓   cup margarine
1   egg, beaten well
½   cup currants
7 to 8   tablespoons light cream
1   egg, beaten well, for egg wash
1   recipe Whipped Honey-Orange Spread (see below)

Note: Instead of shaping individual scones with a biscuit cutter, you can shape dough into an 8-inch round about ½-inch thick. Cut in eighths with a sharp knife, brush with egg wash.

Preheat oven to 400 degrees. Combine flour, sugar, baking powder, and salt in a medium bowl; cut in margarine with a fork or pastry blender until mixture resembles fine crumbs. Stir in beaten egg, currants, and just enough light cream to make dough leave sides of the bowl. Turn dough onto a lightly floured surface. Knead lightly 10 times. Roll ½-inch thick. Cut dough with round biscuit cutter. Place on ungreased cookie sheet. Make egg wash by beating egg; brush tops of scones. Bake until golden brown, about 10 to 12 minutes. Serve hot with Whipped Honey-Orange Spread. Makes 10 to 12 scones.

Whipped Honey-Orange Spread

1   8-ounce package cream cheese
2   tablespoons honey
1   tablespoon orange zest

In small bowl, beat cream cheese, honey, and orange zest until light and fluffy. Store, covered, in refrigerator. Keeps one month.

CRÊPES

3   eggs
½   cup milk
½   cup water
3   tablespoons butter, melted
¾   cup flour
½   teaspoon salt

Combine all ingredients in blender and process about 1 minute. Scrape down sides with rubber spatula and blend about 30 seconds more. Refrigerate for 1 hour. To cook, heat omelet pan, crêpe pan, or skillet over medium-high heat—pan should be just hot enough to sizzle a drop of water. Brush lightly with melted butter. For each crêpe, pour in just enough batter to cover bottom of pan, tipping and tilting pan to move batter quickly over bottom. If crêpe has holes, add a drop or two of batter to patch. Cook until light brown on bottom and dry on top. Remove from pan and stack on plate. Makes 12 crêpes.

Currant-Cream Scones

Pumpkin Cake Roll

3   eggs
1   cup sugar
2/3 cup canned or cooked pumpkin
1   teaspoon lemon juice
3/4 cup flour
1   teaspoon baking powder
2   teaspoons ground cinnamon
1   teaspoon ground ginger
1/2 teaspoon ground nutmeg
1/2 teaspoon salt
1/2 cup chopped nuts
     Powdered sugar
1   recipe Cream Cheese Filling (see below)

Preheat oven to 350 degrees. Line a 10x15-inch jelly roll pan with waxed paper; grease paper. Beat eggs in a large bowl until lemon-colored. Gradually beat in sugar. Stir in pumpkin and lemon juice. In a separate bowl sift together flour, baking powder, cinnamon, ginger, nutmeg, and salt; fold into egg-pumpkin mixture. Pour batter into pan; sprinkle with chopped nuts. Bake for 15 minutes. Sprinkle powdered sugar on a kitchen towel. Turn cake onto towel, and remove waxed paper. Roll up cake and towel lengthwise. Cool in refrigerator or freezer.

When roll is cool, unroll and spread with Cream Cheese Filling. Roll up again (without towel) and wrap in plastic wrap. Makes 10 to 12 servings.

Cream Cheese Filling

2   3-ounce packages cream cheese, softened
1/4 cup butter or margarine, softened
1   cup powdered sugar
1/2 teaspoon vanilla

Whip cream cheese and butter or margarine in a medium bowl until smooth. Beat in powdered sugar and vanilla.

Pantry Lemon Krackle

1 1/2 cups packed brown sugar
1 1/2 cups flour
20   soda crackers, crushed
3/4   teaspoon baking soda
1   cup margarine, softened
3/4   cup chopped nuts
2   cups sugar
1/4   cup cornstarch
       Juice of 4 lemons
4   eggs, beaten well
2   cups water
1/4   cup margarine
1   teaspoon vanilla
       Whipped cream, for topping
       Lemon slices, for garnishing

Preheat oven to 350 degrees. Mix brown sugar, flour, crushed crackers, and baking soda in a large bowl. Cut in 1 cup margarine with a fork or pastry blender until mixture is crumbly. Stir in nuts. Press mixture into bottom of 9x13-inch baking pan; set aside. Make filling by mixing 2 cups sugar with cornstarch in a medium saucepan. Add lemon juice, beaten eggs, and water. Cook and stir over medium heat until thickened, about 6 to 8 minutes. Remove from heat and stir in 1/4 cup margarine and vanilla. Pour filling on top of crust. Bake for 30 minutes. Serve topped with whipped cream and garnished with a lemon slice. Makes 12 servings.

PISTACHIO PUDDING DESSERT

2 cups dry biscuit mix
2 tablespoons brown sugar
1/4 cup margarine
1/2 cup chopped nuts
1 1/2 cups powdered sugar
2 8-ounce packages cream cheese, softened
1/2 pint whipping cream
1 quart milk
2 3.5-ounce packages instant pistachio pudding
Whipped cream and green cherries, for garnishing

Preheat oven to 375 degrees. Combine biscuit mix and brown sugar in a medium bowl; cut in margarine with a pastry blender or fork until crumbly. Add chopped nuts and press into a 9x13-inch baking pan. Bake 10 minutes. Cool on a wire rack. While crust cools, cream powdered sugar and cream cheese in a large bowl until light and fluffy. Whip 1/2 pint cream in a separate bowl, then fold into cream cheese mixture; spread mixture over baked crust. Pour milk into a medium bowl. Add pudding mixes and beat until well blended. Pour over cream cheese layer. Refrigerate until set, about 2 hours. Top each serving with whipped cream and a green cherry. Makes 12 to 15 servings.

CHRISTMAS RASPBERRY CRUNCH

2 cups crushed pretzels
3 tablespoons sugar
1/2 cup butter or margarine
1 8-ounce package cream cheese, softened
1 cup sugar
1 12-ounce carton whipped topping
1 16-ounce can crushed pineapple, drained
1 6-ounce package raspberry gelatin
3 cups boiling water
1 10-ounce bag frozen raspberries
Whipped cream, for garnishing

Preheat oven to 400 degrees. Crush pretzels with rolling pin; combine with sugar and melted butter in a small bowl. Press into bottom of 9x13-inch baking pan. Bake 5 minutes. Cool on a wire rack.

In a large bowl beat cream cheese and sugar until fluffy. Mix in whipped topping, then fold in drained pineapple. Spread mixture onto cooled pretzel crust.

Dissolve gelatin in boiling water. Stir in frozen raspberries and place gelatin in refrigerator until syrupy, about 30 minutes. Pour over cream cheese layer. Refrigerate until set. Garnish with whipped cream. Makes 12 servings.

ZINA'S CARAMEL DUMPLINGS

2 tablespoons butter
1 1/2 cups packed brown sugar
1 1/2 cups water
1 1/4 cups flour
1/2 cup sugar
2 teaspoons baking powder
1/2 teaspoon salt
1/2 cup milk
1 teaspoon vanilla
Cream or vanilla ice cream

Make a caramel sauce by combining butter, brown sugar, and water in a medium saucepan. Bring to a boil, then reduce heat to a simmer. While sauce simmers, make dumplings by mixing flour, sugar, baking powder, and salt in a medium bowl; stir in milk and vanilla (batter should be stiff). Drop by teaspoons into simmering caramel sauce. Cover pan and simmer for 20 minutes. Do not remove lid until time is up. Spoon dumplings into serving dishes and serve with cream or ice cream, if desired. Makes 6 servings.

STEAMED CARROT PUDDING

1¾ cups flour
1½ cups sugar
1½ teaspoons baking soda
½ teaspoon salt
1 teaspoon ground cinnamon
¾ teaspoon ground nutmeg
¼ teaspoon ground cloves
1½ cups grated carrots
1½ cups grated potatoes
¼ cup butter or margarine, melted
1 cup coarsely chopped nuts
1 recipe Butterscotch Sauce (see below)

Note: You can flame this pudding by soaking sugar cubes (one for each serving) in lemon extract, then placing one cube on top of each serving of pudding and lighting just before serving.

Combine all ingredients, except Butterscotch Sauce, in large mixing bowl until well blended. Pour into an 8-cup greased pudding mold or divide into 2 or 3 empty, washed 26- to 28-ounce cans sprayed with non-stick cooking spray, filling two-thirds full. Cover with foil. Fill a roasting pan with 2 inches water. Place a rack in the pan and set pudding mold or cans on top of rack. Cover pan, and steam on low heat on top of stove for 2 hours. Check water level occasionally and add more, if necessary. Serve warm with Butterscotch Sauce. Makes 8 to 10 servings.

Butterscotch Sauce

1½ cups packed brown sugar
⅔ cup light corn syrup
½ cup water
Dash salt
⅔ cup evaporated milk

Combine brown sugar, corn syrup, water, and salt in small saucepan. Heat to boiling, stirring until sugar is dissolved. Continue cooking until a small amount forms a very soft ball in cold water (240 degrees). Remove from heat. Cool slightly, then stir in evaporated milk. Makes 2 cups sauce.

CHOCOLATE-PEPPERMINT DELIGHT

2 cups crushed vanilla wafers
¼ cup margarine, melted
½ cup butter
1½ cups powdered sugar
3 eggs, pasteurized
2 squares (2 ounces) unsweetened chocolate, melted
1 cup whipping cream
8 ounces miniature marshmallows
½ cup crushed peppermint candy

Combine vanilla wafers with melted margarine and press into an 8x8-inch pan; set aside. In a large bowl cream margarine and powdered sugar until fluffy. Add eggs and continue to beat; slowly add chocolate, mixing until combined. Spread mixture on top of vanilla wafers; chill for 45 minutes. Whip cream until stiff; fold in marshmallows and spread over chocolate layer. Sprinkle crushed peppermint candy on top. Refrigerate several hours before serving. Makes 9 servings.

Steamed Carrot Pudding

English Trifle

ENGLISH TRIFLE

2 to 3   cups day old sponge cake or
         vanilla wafers

1   16-ounce can fruit cocktail (or any
      kind of fruit)

1   3-ounce package gelatin (rasp-
      berry, strawberry, or cherry)

1   3-ounce package instant vanilla
      pudding*

2   cups cold milk

2   cups whipping cream
      Chopped nuts, for garnishing
      Grated chocolate, for garnishing
      Maraschino cherries, for
      garnishing

Note: For variety, substitute fruit cocktail with fresh or frozen fruit, such as berries, peaches, mangos, and so on.

Line the bottom of a glass serving bowl or trifle dish with the pieces of sponge cake or vanilla wafers. Drain the fruit and arrange atop the cake. Make gelatin according to package directions, and while still warm, pour over cake and fruit. Refrigerate until set, about 2 hours. Beat vanilla pudding powder into cold milk; pour over set gelatin. Cover with plastic wrap and refrigerate. When ready to serve, whip cream and spread over top of pudding. Decorate with chopped nuts, grated chocolate, and maraschino cherries. Makes 8 to 10 servings.

*For a true English trifle, in place of the pudding use Bird's Custard powder, which is available at many food stores in the gourmet or imported foods section. Prepare according to directions on package.

FROSTY VANILLA ICE CREAM

4   Junket tablets

¼   cup cold water

2   quarts milk

2   cups whipping cream

2   cups sugar

⅛   teaspoon salt

4   teaspoons vanilla

Note: Turn this ice cream into a fruity treat by adding 2 cups mashed fresh or thawed frozen fruit, such as raspberries, strawberries, peaches, or boysenberries.

Dissolve Junket tablets in cold water in a small bowl. Mix milk, cream, sugar, and salt in a large saucepan and heat to lukewarm (110 to 115 degrees) over medium heat. Add dissolved Junket tablets and vanilla. Pour mixture into ice cream freezer can; put dasher in place and let stand 10 minutes to set. Freeze according to manufacturer's directions. Makes 4 quarts.

HARVEST PEACH ICE CREAM

8   large ripe peaches
      Juice of 2 lemons

3   cups sugar

2   cups whipping cream

1   14-ounce can sweetened condensed
      milk

1   quart milk

Peel and mash peaches. Combine mashed peaches, lemon juice, and sugar in a large bowl and refrigerate 2 hours. Whip cream; fold into peach mixture with sweetened condensed milk and regular milk. Pour mixture into a 4-quart ice cream freezer and freeze according to manufacturer's directions. Makes 4 quarts.

Ginger Cookies, Jingle Bell Cookie Wreaths,
Grandma's Christmas Bell Cookies

JINGLE BELL COOKIE WREATHS

1   cup sugar
1   cup margarine, softened
1   egg
1½   teaspoons almond extract
3½   cups flour
1   teaspoon baking powder
¼   teaspoon salt
½   cup milk
     Green food coloring
     Cinnamon candies

Cream sugar and margarine in a large bowl. Add egg and almond extract, beating until fluffy. In a separate bowl sift together flour, baking powder, and salt; add to creamed mixture alternately with milk. Divide dough in half; tint half green (about 5 drops of food coloring), leaving other half white. Chill dough for 1 hour.

Preheat oven to 375 degrees. Sprinkle sugar on work surface. For each wreath, shape 1 teaspoon white dough and 1 teaspoon green dough into two 4-inch ropes. Twist ropes together and shape into wreath. Place on ungreased cookie sheets; press 2 or 3 cinnamon candies on each wreath to look like holly berries. Bake 9 to 12 minutes, or until light golden around the edges. Cool on wire rack. Store in covered container. Makes about 4 dozen wreaths.

GRANDMA'S CHRISTMAS BELL COOKIES

2   cups butter or margarine, softened
1½   cups sugar
2   eggs
1   teaspoon vanilla
5   cups flour
1   teaspoon baking powder
½   teaspoon salt

Cream butter and sugar in a large bowl. Add eggs and vanilla and beat until fluffy. Sift together flour, baking powder, and salt, and add to creamed mixture. Refrigerate dough until chilled, about 1 hour.

Preheat oven to 350 degrees. Roll out dough ¼-inch thick on a lightly floured board or pastry cloth. Cut with bell-shaped cookie cutter. Place on greased cookie sheets and bake for 12 to 15 minutes. Cool on wire rack. Frost with red- or green-tinted powdered sugar icing. Store in covered container. Makes 5 dozen cookies.

JOLLY JUMBO OATMEAL COOKIES

1   cup shortening or margarine
1   cup packed brown sugar
1   cup white sugar
3   eggs
1   teaspoon vanilla
2   cups flour
1   teaspoon baking soda
1/2 teaspoon salt
1   teaspoon ground cinnamon
1/2 teaspoon ground cloves
1/2 teaspoon ground ginger
3   cups quick-cooking oats
1   cup walnuts, chopped

Note: For variety, add raisins, chocolate chips, cut-up gumdrops, or M&Ms candies to dough and bake as directed.

Preheat oven to 350 degrees. Cream shortening and sugars in a large bowl until fluffy. Beat in eggs, then vanilla. In a separate bowl sift together flour, baking soda, salt, cinnamon, cloves, and ginger; add gradually to creamed mixture. Stir in oatmeal and nuts. Measure ¼ cup dough for each cookie and place on greased cookie sheets, about 4 inches apart. Bake 13 to 15 minutes, until light brown. Carefully remove from cookie sheet. Cool on wire racks. Store in covered container. Makes 2 dozen cookies.

MILLION-DOLLAR COOKIES

2   cups shortening
1   cup white sugar
1   cup packed brown sugar
2   eggs
1   teaspoon vanilla
1   teaspoon almond extract
4   cups flour
2   teaspoons baking soda
2   teaspoons cream of tartar

Note: You can also add chocolate chips, chopped nuts, or raisins to batter before chilling. When ready to bake, drop by spoonfuls onto greased cookie sheets and bake as directed.

Cream shortening, sugars, eggs, vanilla, and almond extract in a large bowl until light and fluffy. In a separate bowl sift together flour, baking soda, and cream of tartar; add gradually to creamed mixture. Chill dough for 1 hour.

Preheat oven to 350 degrees. Mold dough into 1-inch balls. Place onto greased cookie sheets. Flatten each cookie with bottom of a drinking glass that has been dipped in sugar. Bake 10 minutes. Cool on wire rack. Store in covered container. Makes 5 dozen cookies.

THORA'S BUTTERSCOTCH COOKIES

1/2 cup butter or margarine, softened
1 1/2 cups packed brown sugar
2 eggs
1 teaspoon vanilla
2 2/3 cups flour
1 teaspoon baking soda
1/2 teaspoon baking powder
1/2 teaspoon salt
1 cup sour cream
1 cup chopped pecans
Pecan halves
1 recipe Butterscotch Frosting (see below)

Preheat oven to 350 degrees. Cream butter and brown sugar in a large bowl until fluffy; add eggs and vanilla and beat well. In a separate bowl sift together flour, baking soda, baking powder, and salt; add to creamed mixture alternately with sour cream, mixing after each addition. Fold in chopped pecans. Drop by spoonfuls onto greased cookie sheets. Bake 20 minutes. Cool on wire rack. Frost with Butterscotch Frosting and top each cookie with a pecan half. Makes 5 dozen cookies.

Butterscotch Frosting

1/2 cup butter
3 cups powdered sugar
1/4 cup hot water

Cook butter in saucepan over medium heat until bubbly and golden brown, about 2 minutes. Beat in powdered sugar and hot water until frosting is smooth and creamy. Allow to cool slightly and spread on cookies.

PEANUT BUTTER COOKIES

5 1/4 cups all-purpose flour
2 teaspoons soda
1 teaspoon salt
1 cup butter
3/4 cup shortening
1 1/4 cups sugar
1 1/4 cups packed brown sugar
4 eggs
1 teaspoon vanilla
3/4 cup peanut butter

Preheat oven to 350 degrees. Line a cookie sheet with waxed paper and set aside. Mix flour, soda, and salt together in a medium bowl and set aside. Cream together butter, shortening, sugar, brown sugar, eggs, and vanilla in a large mixing bowl. Then stir in peanut butter. Add flour mixture and stir until well blended. Drop dough by tablespoonfuls onto cookie sheets. Using a fork dipped in flour, flatten each cookie slightly in a crisscross pattern. Bake for 8 to 10 minutes or until slightly golden around the edges. Do not overbake. Makes 5 dozen 3-inch cookies.

TURTLE COOKIES

½   cup margarine, softened

¾   cup sugar

2   eggs

6   tablespoons cocoa

1   teaspoon vanilla

1   cup flour

1   recipe Turtle Frosting (see below)

Note: Turn these into a peanut butter treat by decreasing the amount of margarine to ¼ cup and adding ½ cup peanut butter.

Heat a standard waffle iron. Cream margarine and sugar in a large bowl until light and fluffy. Beat in eggs, cocoa, and vanilla. Add flour and beat until incorporated. Drop by teaspoonfuls onto a hot waffle iron; cook 1 minute. Cook 4 to 6 cookies at a time, depending on the size of the waffle iron. Remove from iron and frost with Turtle Frosting. Makes 18 to 20 cookies.

Turtle Frosting

½   cup light corn syrup

1   tablespoon cocoa

2½   tablespoons margarine

¼   cup cold water

½   cup sugar

½   teaspoon vanilla

2   cups powdered sugar

Place all ingredients except vanilla and powdered sugar in a medium saucepan and bring to a boil. Boil for 3 minutes. Remove from heat and let stand a few minutes to cool. Add vanilla and powdered sugar and beat with an electric mixer until smooth.

CHERRY MACAROON COOKIES

1½   cups sugar

1⅓   cups shortening

2   eggs

½   teaspoon almond extract

1   teaspoon salt

3½   cups flour

2   teaspoons baking powder

2   teaspoons baking soda

1   cup maraschino cherries, cut up

1½   cups flaked coconut

Preheat oven to 375 degrees. Cream sugar and shortening in a large bowl until light and fluffy. Add eggs, almond extract, and salt; mix well. In a separate bowl sift together flour, baking powder, and baking soda; add to creamed mixture. Stir in cherries and flaked coconut and mix well. Dough will be quite stiff. Drop by spoonfuls onto ungreased cookie sheets. Bake 8 to 10 minutes, until lightly golden brown. Makes 36 cookies.

NORTH POLE NUGGETS

1/2 cup butter, softened
1/2 cup shortening
1/2 cup sugar
1 teaspoon almond extract
2 cups sifted flour
Red and green maraschino cherries

Preheat oven to 350 degrees. Cream butter, shortening, and sugar in a large bowl. Add almond extract and flour; blend well. Shape dough into balls, using 1 tablespoon dough for each cookie. Place on greased cookie sheets. Make indentation in center of each cookie and press maraschino cherry into top. Bake 8 to 10 minutes. Cool on wire rack. Store in covered container. Makes 2½ dozen cookies.

SODA CRACKER COOKIES

35 saltine crackers
1 cup packed brown sugar
1 cup butter
2 cups chocolate chips
1/2 cup chopped nuts

Preheat oven to 350 degrees. Line a 15x10-inch jelly roll pan with foil or parchment paper; grease the foil. Line the pan with saltines, placed as close together as possible. Combine sugar and butter in a small saucepan and bring to a boil, stirring often. Boil for 2½ minutes, stirring constantly. Pour butter sauce over crackers. Place coated saltines in pre-heated oven for 5 minutes. Remove from oven and sprinkle chocolate chips on top. When the chips are melted, spread chocolate over cookies and sprinkle with nuts. Cool and cut or break into small squares. Makes 3 dozen cookies.

HONEY CHOCOLATE DROPS

1 cup shortening
2/3 cup honey
2 eggs, slightly beaten
1 teaspoon baking soda
1/4 cup water
2 teaspoons vanilla
2 2/3 cups flour
1 teaspoon salt
1 cup chocolate chips
1/2 cup chopped walnuts

Preheat oven to 375 degrees. Cream shortening and honey in a large bowl until blended. Add eggs and beat until fluffy. Dissolve baking soda in 1/4 cup water in a small bowl and beat into mixture, followed by vanilla. Sift together flour and salt and add to mixture. Mix in chocolate chips and nuts. Drop by spoonfuls onto ungreased cookie sheets. Bake 10 minutes. Cool on wire racks. Store in covered container. Makes 4 dozen cookies.

CHOCOLATE ORANGE LOGS

1 cup butter or margarine, softened
1/2 cup sifted powdered sugar
1 teaspoon orange zest
1 teaspoon orange extract
2 cups flour
1 cup chocolate chips
1/2 cup finely chopped nuts

Preheat oven to 350 degrees. Cream butter in a large bowl, gradually adding sugar and beating until light and fluffy. Stir in orange zest and orange extract. Gradually add flour. Shape dough into a long roll 3/4-inch wide; cut roll into 2-inch pieces. Place on greased cookie sheet. Flatten one end of each cookie lengthwise with fork. Bake 10 minutes, or until light brown. Cool cookies on wire rack. Melt chocolate chips in microwave oven or in top of double boiler over simmering water. Dip unflattened ends of cookies in chocolate; then roll in chopped nuts. Store in covered container. Makes 4 dozen cookies.

KRIS KRINKLES

1/2 cup shortening
1 2/3 cups sugar
2 eggs
2 teaspoons vanilla
2 squares (2 ounces) unsweetened chocolate, melted
2 1/4 cups sifted flour
1 teaspoon salt
1/3 cup milk
1/2 cup chopped walnuts
Sifted powdered sugar

Cream shortening and sugar in a large bowl until light and fluffy. Add eggs and vanilla and beat well. Fold in melted chocolate. In a separate bowl sift together flour and salt; add to chocolate mixture alternately with milk, stirring after each addition. Stir in nuts. Chill thoroughly 3 to 4 hours or overnight.

Preheat oven to 350 degrees. Form into 1-inch balls and roll each ball lightly in powdered sugar. Place on greased cookie sheets 2 to 3 inches apart. Bake 12 to 15 minutes. Cool slightly before removing from pan. Continue cooling on wire rack. Makes 45 cookies.

GINGER COOKIES

3/4 cup shortening
1 cup sugar
1/4 cup molasses
1 egg
2 cups flour
2 teaspoons baking soda
1/4 teaspoon salt
1 1/2 teaspoons ground ginger
1 teaspoon ground cinnamon

Cream shortening and sugar in a large bowl. Add molasses and egg and beat well. In a separate bowl sift together flour, baking soda, salt, ginger, and cinnamon; add gradually to creamed mixture, mixing well. Chill dough for 30 minutes.

Preheat oven to 350 degrees. Mold dough into 1-inch balls. Place on lightly greased cookie sheets and bake 8 to 10 minutes. Don't overbake. Cool on wire rack. Store in covered container. Makes 4 dozen cookies.

Chocolate Orange Logs, Kris Krinkles,
Date Pinwheels, Honey Chocolate Drops

DATE PINWHEELS

Irresistible Cookies and Sweets

2 cups chopped dates
1 cup white sugar
1 cup water
1 cup chopped nuts
1 cup margarine, softened
2 cups packed brown sugar
3 eggs
4 cups flour
½ teaspoon salt
½ teaspoon baking soda

Mix dates, white sugar, and water together in a small saucepan and cook 10 minutes over medium heat. Stir in nuts and set aside to cool.

In a large mixing bowl, cream margarine and brown sugar. Beat in eggs. In a separate bowl sift together flour, salt, and baking soda; stir into creamed mixture (dough will be stiff). Divide dough in half and chill 1 hour, or until dough can be rolled easily.

On lightly floured surface, roll dough out into two 10x15-inch rectangles. Spread each rectangle with half of the cooled date filling. Carefully roll up jelly-roll style, beginning at long side. Wrap each roll in waxed paper and refrigerate several hours.

Preheat oven to 375 degrees. Cut chilled rolls into ¼-inch slices. Place on greased cookie sheets. Bake 12 minutes. Remove from cookie sheet and cool on wire rack. Store in covered container. Makes 6 dozen cookies.

DANISH SHORTBREAD

2 cups butter, softened
1 cup sugar
  Pinch salt
4 scant cups sifted flour
1 egg, beaten well
  Chopped almonds

Preheat oven to 375 degrees. Cream butter, sugar, and salt in a large bowl until light and fluffy, about 7 to 10 minutes. Gradually add flour, ½ cup at a time, beating after each addition. Roll out dough about ½-inch thick on floured board or pastry cloth. Cut dough lengthwise in 1-inch strips. Then cut strips on an angle into 2-inch lengths; place on ungreased cookie sheets. Press each cookie down slightly with back of fingers. Brush tops with beaten egg. Sprinkle with chopped almonds. Bake 20 minutes or until light brown. Cool on wire rack. Store in covered container. Makes 3 dozen cookies.

BRUNE KAGER (BROWN CHRISTMAS COOKIES)

1   cup butter or margarine
1   cup packed brown sugar
1   cup dark corn syrup
4   cups sifted flour
1   teaspoon baking soda
1/2   teaspoon salt
1   teaspoon cardamom
1   teaspoon ground cloves
1/2   teaspoon ground allspice
1   teaspoon ground cinnamon
1   tablespoon orange zest
    Slivered blanched almonds, for
      garnishing

Note: Make this dough a few weeks in advance and store in the refrigerator, where the flavors will blend and intensify.

Melt butter in a small saucepan; add sugar and corn syrup. Remove from heat. Pour mixture into a large bowl. In a medium bowl combine flour, soda, salt, and spices. Pour dry mixture into butter-sugar mixture and mix well. Stir in orange zest. Mold dough into two long rolls, each about 15 inches long. Refrigerate up to three weeks before baking. When ready to bake, cut dough into thin slices and place slices on greased cookie sheets. Decorate each cookie with blanched almonds. Bake at 375 degrees for 8 minutes. Cool on wire rack. Store in tightly covered container. Makes 10 dozen cookies.

GINGERBREAD BOY ORNAMENTS

1   recipe Brune Kager dough (see
      above)
    Whole cloves
    Raisins
    Ribbon, for threading and hanging
      ornaments

Preheat oven to 350 degrees. Follow recipe for Brune Kager. After dough is mixed, turn out onto lightly floured surface and roll dough to 1/4-inch thickness. Using gingerbread boy cookie cutter, cut out cookies. Place on greased cookie sheets. Press in 2 whole cloves for eyes and 2 or 3 raisins for buttons. Use a straw or ice pick to poke a hole in the top of the cookie. Bake for 15 minutes. Cool on wire rack. Thread ribbon through hole and hang cookies in window or on Christmas tree. Makes 3 to 4 dozen cookies, depending on the size of cookie cutter.

UNBAKED DATE-NUT ROLL

1/2   pound graham crackers
1/2   pound miniature marshmallows
1/2   cup nuts, chopped (walnuts,
      almonds, or pecans)
1/2   pound dates, cut in small pieces
1   cup cream
    Whipped cream, for garnishing

Crush graham crackers with rolling pin; set aside about 1/4 of the crumbs. Mix marshmallows, nuts, and dates with remaining 3/4 of graham cracker crumbs. Add cream to moisten. Mold into a long roll; then roll in reserved crumbs. Wrap in wax paper and refrigerate. When ready to serve, slice and garnish with whipped cream. Makes 8 servings.

CATHY'S BROWNIES

1	cup butter or margarine
½	cup cocoa
4	eggs
2	cups sugar
1	teaspoon vanilla
1½	cups flour
½	teaspoon salt
½	teaspoon baking soda
¾	cup chopped nuts
1	recipe Chocolate Frosting (see below)

Note: Turn regular brownies into a sundae treat by placing an unfrosted brownie on each dessert plate. Top brownie with a scoop of vanilla ice cream; drizzle with chocolate sauce and add a dollop of whipped cream and a green or red cherry. Garnish with a sprig of holly (optional).

Preheat oven to 350 degrees. Grease a 9x13-inch baking pan. Melt butter in a small saucepan over medium heat; stir in cocoa and set aside to cool. Beat eggs in a large bowl, then gradually add sugar, a little at a time. Add vanilla and melted chocolate mixture, stirring until smooth. In a separate bowl sift together flour, salt, and baking soda; add to chocolate mixture. Stir in nuts. Pour into prepared pan and bake about 30 minutes, or until wooden toothpick inserted in center of brownies comes out clean. Cool on a wire rack. Pour Chocolate Frosting over cooked brownies and spread lightly. When frosting is firm, cut into bars. Makes 2 dozen brownies.

Chocolate Frosting

¼	cup cocoa
¼	cup butter or margarine
5	tablespoons milk
3	cups powdered sugar

Melt butter in a large saucepan over medium heat; stir in cocoa. Add milk, then beat in powdered sugar until frosting reaches spreading consistency.

RASPBERRY BARS

1¼	cups flour
1	teaspoon baking powder
	Pinch salt
3	tablespoons packed brown sugar
½	cup butter or margarine
1	cup (4 ounces) grated cheddar cheese
1	cup raspberry jam
½	cup chopped walnuts or almonds

Preheat oven to 350 degrees. In a medium bowl, combine flour, baking powder, salt, and brown sugar; cut in butter or margarine with a pastry blender or fork until mixture resembles coarse crumbs. Stir in cheese. Remove ¾ cup of the mixture. Press remaining mixture evenly in the bottom of an ungreased 8x8-inch pan. Spread jam evenly over crust. Sprinkle on nuts then remaining crumb mixture. Press down gently. Bake 25 minutes or until golden brown. Cool in pan and cut into bars. Store in refrigerator. Makes 12 bars.

LAYERED CREAM CHEESE BROWNIES

1	8-ounce package cream cheese, softened
1/3	cup sugar
1	egg
1 to 2	tablespoons milk
1	cup water
1	cup margarine
5	tablespoons cocoa
2	ounces (2 squares) unsweetened baking chocolate
4	eggs
2	cups sugar
1/2	cup buttermilk
1	teaspoon baking soda
1	teaspoon vanilla
3	cups flour
1	recipe Cream Cheese Icing (see below)

Preheat oven to 350 degrees. Grease a 12x17-inch cookie sheet. In a medium bowl beat cream cheese, 1/3 cup sugar, 1 egg, and milk until fluffy; set aside.

In a small saucepan, heat water, margarine, cocoa, and chocolate over medium heat until melted; set aside. In a large mixing bowl, beat eggs and sugar until light and well combined. Mix in melted chocolate mixture, then add buttermilk, baking soda, vanilla, and flour; mix well. Pour half of batter onto the greased cookie sheet. Spoon cream cheese mixture evenly over top of batter. Pour remaining chocolate batter over cream cheese. Bake 30 minutes. Remove from oven and cool on wire rack. Spread with Cream Cheese Icing. Makes 42 2x2½-inch brownies.

Cream Cheese Icing

1	3-ounce package cream cheese, softened
1/4	cup margarine, softened
3	cups powdered sugar
3	tablespoons cocoa
1	teaspoon vanilla
1 to 2	tablespoons milk

Make icing by whipping cream cheese and margarine in a medium bowl until fluffy; beat in powdered sugar, cocoa, and vanilla with a little milk until icing reaches spreading consistency. Spread over cooled brownies.

BUTTER PECAN SQUARES

1/2	cup butter, softened
1/2	cup packed brown sugar
1	egg
1	teaspoon vanilla
3/4	cup flour
2	cups milk chocolate chips
3/4	cup chopped pecans

Preheat oven to 350 degrees. Grease an 8x8-inch baking pan. Cream butter, sugar, egg, and vanilla in a large bowl until light and fluffy. Blend in flour. Stir in 1 cup of the chocolate chips and ½ cup pecans. Pour into baking dish. Bake 25 to 30 minutes. Remove from oven and immediately sprinkle with remaining 1 cup chips. When chips melt, spread evenly over top with knife. Sprinkle with remaining pecans. Cool, then cut into squares. Makes 16 bars.

OATMEAL FUDGE BARS

1 cup margarine, softened
2 cups packed brown sugar
2 eggs
2 teaspoons vanilla
2½ cups flour
1 teaspoon baking soda
½ teaspoon salt
1½ cups quick-cooking oats
1 14-ounce can sweetened condensed milk
1 12-ounce package semisweet chocolate chips
¼ cup margarine
2 teaspoons vanilla
1 cup chopped walnuts (optional)

Preheat oven to 350 degrees. Grease a 9x13-inch baking pan and set aside. Cream margarine and brown sugar in a large bowl; beat in eggs and 2 teaspoons vanilla. In a separate bowl sift together flour, baking soda, and salt; add to creamed mixture. Stir in oats and set aside.

In a heavy saucepan combine sweetened condensed milk, chocolate chips, and ¼ cup margarine. Heat over low heat until chocolate is melted, stirring occasionally. Remove from heat and stir in 2 teaspoons vanilla and nuts.

Spread two-thirds of oats mixture into prepared baking pan and press down. Spread melted chocolate mixture over top. Drop remaining one-third oats mixture on top by small spoonfuls. Bake 25 minutes, until top looks light brown. Cool, then cut into bars. Makes 36 bars.

LION HOUSE PECAN BARS

¾ cup butter or margarine
¾ cup white sugar
2 eggs
3 cups flour
½ teaspoon baking powder
Zest of 1 lemon
1 cup butter or margarine
1 cup packed brown sugar
1 cup honey
¼ cup light cream
3 cups pecans, chopped

Preheat oven to 375 degrees. Grease a 9x13-inch pan. Cream ¾ cup butter and white sugar in a large bowl until light and fluffy; add eggs and beat well. Blend in flour, baking powder, and lemon zest. Press dough into a greased 9x13-inch pan. Prick dough with fork. Bake 12 to 15 minutes, then remove from oven.

Make a butter-pecan topping by combining 1 cup butter, brown sugar, and honey in a medium saucepan over medium to medium-high heat. Bring to a boil, then cook and stir 5 minutes. Cool slightly and add cream and chopped pecans. Spread over partially baked crust. Reduce oven temperature to 350 degrees and return bars to oven; bake 30 to 35 minutes. Cool and cut into bars. Makes 24 small bars.

PEANUT BUTTER FINGERS

½ cup butter or margarine, softened
½ cup white sugar
½ cup packed brown sugar
1 egg
⅓ cup peanut butter
½ teaspoon baking soda
¼ teaspoon salt
½ teaspoon vanilla
1 cup flour
1 cup quick-cooking oats
½ cup sifted powdered sugar
¼ cup peanut butter
1 to 2 tablespoons milk
1 cup chocolate chips

Preheat oven to 350 degrees. Grease a 9x13-inch baking pan. Cream butter with white and brown sugars in a large bowl. Blend in egg, ⅓ cup peanut butter, baking soda, salt, and vanilla. Stir in flour and oats. Pour into prepared pan and bake for 20 to 25 minutes, until golden brown.

While bars are baking, prepare topping by creaming powdered sugar, ¼ cup peanut butter, and enough milk to make an acceptable spreading consistency.

Remove pan from oven and sprinkle bars with chocolate chips. Let stand 5 minutes, then smooth over top of bars. With knife or spatula, swirl topping over melted chocolate. Cool thoroughly, then cut into 24 bars.

JOLLY ELF GRANOLA BARS

1 14 ounce package chocolate caramels
2 tablespoons water
¾ cup crunchy peanut butter
3 cups plain granola
1 cup golden raisins
½ cup salted peanuts

Note: You may substitute plain caramels for chocolate caramels.

Butter a 9x13-inch baking pan. Melt caramels and water over medium heat in heavy saucepan, stirring often (or melt in glass dish in microwave oven). Remove from heat and stir in peanut butter. Add granola, raisins, and peanuts; mix well. Pour into pan and let cool. Cut into 1x2-inch bars. Makes about 32 bars.

COCONUT CHEWS

1 cup flour
2 tablespoons white sugar
   Pinch salt
½ cup butter
1½ cups packed brown sugar
2 eggs
2 teaspoons vanilla
1 cup flaked coconut
1 cup chopped nuts

Preheat oven to 350 degrees. Combine flour, white sugar, and salt in a medium bowl; cut in butter with a pastry blender or fork until mixture resembles coarse crumbs. Press mixture into an 8x12-inch baking pan. Bake 15 minutes. While crust is baking, beat brown sugar and eggs together in a medium bowl until smooth. Mix in vanilla, coconut, and nuts. Carefully spread over baked crust, then return to oven and continue baking 25 minutes longer. Cut into squares while warm. Cool, then cover pan to store. Makes 24 bars.

OLD-FASHIONED FUDGE

3   cups sugar
3   tablespoons cocoa
3   tablespoons light corn syrup
1   cup light cream
2   tablespoons butter
1   teaspoon vanilla
$^1/_2$ cup nuts

Butter an 8x8-inch pan; set aside. Combine sugar, cocoa, corn syrup, and cream in a heavy saucepan. Cook and stir over medium heat until mixture starts to boil. Stir occasionally, until just a little past soft-ball stage (just over 236 degrees on the candy thermometer; mixture will form a soft ball after being dropped in cold water). Remove from heat and add butter and vanilla, but don't stir. Cool to about 110 degrees, which could take 40 or 50 minutes, then beat with a wooden spoon until candy loses its gloss and thickens. Add nuts and pour into prepared pan. Cool, then cut into small squares. Makes 48 to 64 pieces of candy.

LUSCIOUS FUDGE

1   12-ounce milk chocolate bar,
       broken into pieces
2   cups semisweet chocolate chips
1   7-ounce jar marshmallow crème
1   12-ounce can evaporated milk
4$^1/_2$ cups sugar
$^1/_8$ teaspoon salt
2   teaspoons vanilla
2   cups chopped walnuts

Butter a 9x13-inch pan. Combine milk chocolate bar pieces, chocolate chips, and marshmallow crème in large mixing bowl; set aside. In a heavy saucepan, combine evaporated milk, sugar, and salt. Bring to a boil over medium heat and boil for six minutes. Pour over chocolate mixture. Beat vigorously with wooden spoon until creamy. Add vanilla and chopped walnuts. Mix well. Pour into prepared pan. Let stand two hours, then cut into small squares. Makes 5 pounds of candy.

CREAMY THREE-NUT CANDY

3   cups sugar
1   cup light corn syrup
2   cups heavy cream
2   cups walnuts
2   cups pecans
2   cups Brazil nuts, broken into pieces

Butter two 4$^1/_2$ x 8-inch loaf pans. In a large, heavy saucepan combine all ingredients and place over low heat. Cook and stir constantly until mixture reaches soft-ball stage, 236 degrees (a soft ball should form when mixture is dropped into cold water). Allow 30 to 40 minutes for cooking. Remove from heat. While candy is still warm, stir until creamy and mixture begins to thicken. Pour into prepared pans and pack down. Let harden. Remove from container, wrap in foil, and store in an air-tight container in refrigerator. Slice paper thin to serve. Makes 4$^1/_2$ pounds of candy. This keeps a long time, 4 to 6 weeks.

Aunt Bill's Brown Candy

3   cups sugar
1   cup light cream
1/4   teaspoon baking soda
1/4   cup butter
1/8   teaspoon salt
1   teaspoon vanilla
1/2   cup chopped pecans

Put 1 cup sugar in a heavy skillet and place on low heat. Stir continuously until sugar caramelizes and turns light brown; set aside. Combine the remaining 2 cups sugar and the cream in a heavy saucepan and place over low heat. Slowly pour the caramelized sugar in a fine stream into the sugar and cream mixture, stirring constantly. Cook and stir over low heat until mixture reaches firm-ball stage, 245 degrees (mixture forms a firm ball when dropped into cold water and won't flatten when removed). Remove from heat and immediately add baking soda, stirring vigorously. Add butter and salt and let stand 20 minutes. Add vanilla and beat, using a wooden spoon, until mixture is thick and heavy and loses its glossy sheen. Add chopped nuts and turn into a buttered 9x13-inch pan. When slightly cool, cut into squares. Candy will stay moist indefinitely if stored in covered container in refrigerator. Makes 2 pounds of candy.

Holiday Divinity

3   cups sugar
1   cup light corn syrup
1/2   cup water
2   egg whites, at room temperature
1   teaspoon vanilla
    Red food coloring
1/3   cup chopped maraschino cherries
1/2   cup chopped pecans

Combine sugar, corn syrup, and water in a heavy saucepan and bring to a boil. Cover pan for 3 minutes to allow the steam inside the pan to melt the sugar crystals down from sides of pan. Remove cover. Cook without stirring until syrup reaches hard-ball stage, 260 degrees (when dropped in cold water, mixture forms a hard ball that is difficult to mold when removed from water). While syrup is cooking, place egg whites in a large bowl and beat until stiff peaks form. When syrup is done, pour over egg whites in a fine stream, beating vigorously. Do not scrape pan. Add vanilla and 2 or 3 drops of red food coloring to tint pink. Continue beating until candy is thick and creamy and holds its shape. Stir in cherries and pecans. Drop from a teaspoon onto waxed paper. Divinity does not keep well, so serve while fresh. Makes about 4 dozen pieces.

PEANUT BRITTLE

1½   cups sugar
½   cup light corn syrup
¼   cup water
2   cups shelled raw peanuts
1 to 1½   teaspoons baking soda
¼   teaspoon salt

Combine sugar, corn syrup, and water in a heavy saucepan and bring to a boil over medium high heat, stirring often. Gradually stir in peanuts, without losing the boil. Adjust temperature to maintain a rolling boil until the peanuts pop and turn golden brown; remove from heat. Add baking soda, stirring well (the candy will foam up and turn golden brown). Add salt and stir well. Pour on a well-greased platter or cookie sheet. Allow room for candy to spread. (If you like thick peanut brittle let it spread on its own; if you like thinner brittle, spread it a little with the back of a wooden spoon.) When cold, break into chunks. Makes 2 pounds.

CHOCOLATE ALMOND BALLS

1   8-ounce chocolate bar with almonds
1   8-ounce tub frozen whipped topping, thawed to room temperature
30   vanilla wafers, crushed

Note: For variety, roll balls in candy sprinkles, coconut, or chopped nuts.

Melt chocolate bar in top of a double boiler. Cool slightly (don't let it become cold). Stir in thawed whipped topping. Using heaping teaspoonfuls of candy, shape into balls and roll in vanilla wafer crumbs. Keep in freezer for two hours before serving. Store in freezer. Makes about 4 dozen.

HONEY TAFFY POPCORN

1   cup sugar
½   cup light honey
½   cup cream
⅛   teaspoon baking soda
1   teaspoon vanilla
4   quarts popped corn, lightly salted and buttered

Combine sugar, honey, and cream in a heavy saucepan and bring to a boil over medium heat. Adjust temperature to maintain a steady boil and cook to 269 degrees. Remove from heat and stir in baking soda, stirring until bubbles subside (syrup will turn a light golden color); add vanilla. Pour over popped corn, stirring until coated. Cool and break into chunks. Makes 12 servings.

Honey Taffy Popcorn, English Toffee,
Chocolate Almond Balls

QUICK CARAMEL CORN

2 gallons popped corn (1 cup unpopped)
1/2 cup butter
2 cups packed brown sugar
1/2 cup light corn syrup
1 tablespoon water
Pinch baking soda

Place popped corn in a large pan; set aside. Melt butter in saucepan. Add brown sugar, corn syrup, and water. Cook and stir until mixture reaches a hard boil. Add a pinch of baking soda. Remove from heat and pour over popcorn. Stir to coat thoroughly. Cool; then break into clusters. Store in covered container. Makes 12 to 18 servings.

RAZZLE DAZZLE

9 1/2 cups Rice Krispies® cereal
8 1/2 cups Rice Chex® cereal
7 cups Corn Chex® cereal
4 1/2 cups Wheat Chex® cereal
1 10-ounce bag stick pretzels
2 1/2 cups slivered almonds, slightly toasted*
2 cups brown sugar
1 cup white sugar
1 cup light corn syrup
1 cup butter
1 pint (2 cups) cream
Dash salt

Mix the cereals, pretzels, and almonds in a large roasting pan; set aside. Combine sugars, corn syrup, butter, cream, and salt in a heavy saucepan. Bring mixture to a boil over medium heat. Adjust temperature to maintain a steady boil and cook, stirring constantly, to firm-ball stage, 245 degrees (mixture forms a firm ball when dropped into cold water and won't flatten when removed).

Pour cooked syrup over cereals and stir gently until coated. Pour on cookie sheets or table lined with waxed paper until dry. Makes 10 to 12 servings.

* To lightly toast almonds, toss almonds with 1 teaspoon melted butter and spread out on a baking sheet. Bake at 300 degrees, stirring often, for 10 to 15 minutes.

POPCORN-NUT CRUNCH

3 quarts popped corn
1⅓ cups pecan halves
⅔ cup whole almonds (blanched or raw)
½ cup light corn syrup
1⅓ cups sugar
1 cup butter
½ teaspoon cream of tartar
1 tablespoon vanilla
1 teaspoon baking soda
4 cups miniature marshmallows, frozen

Mix popcorn, pecans, and almonds in a large bowl or pan; set aside. In a heavy saucepan, combine corn syrup, sugar, butter, and cream of tartar. Cook and stir over medium-high heat until mixture comes to a boil. Reduce heat to medium and maintain a steady boil for 10 minutes, until mixture reaches hard-ball stage, 260 degrees (when dropped in cold water, mixture forms a hard ball that is difficult to mold when removed from water); remove from heat. Stir in vanilla and baking soda. Pour over popcorn and nuts, stirring to coat evenly. Add frozen marshmallows and continue stirring until mixture is evenly coated with syrup. Spread on buttered cookie sheets to cool. Break into chunks and store in an airtight container. Makes 12 servings.

MOLDED ANIMAL LOLLIPOPS

2 cups sugar
⅔ cup water
⅓ cup light corn syrup
½ teaspoon oil-based flavoring, such as cinnamon, peppermint, or fruit
Food coloring

Note: If you don't have sucker molds, you can place wooden sticks on a greased cookie sheet and pour about 1 tablespoon syrup on the end of each stick to make round lollipops. While candy is still hot and sticky, decorate with gumdrops cut in pieces, cinnamon candies, commercial cake decorations, or frosting.

Coat animal-shaped lollipop molds with nonstick cooking spray and arrange them on a cookie sheet that has also been sprayed. Combine sugar, water, and corn syrup in a heavy saucepan. Cook over high heat, stirring until sugar dissolves and mixture comes to a boil. Reduce heat and continue cooking to hard-crack stage, 300 degrees (when dropped in cold water, mixture should form hard, brittle threads that break easily). Remove from heat and stir in flavoring and coloring. Spoon syrup into lollipop molds; insert wooden sticks; set aside to cool. When lollipops are cool, wrap in plastic wrap. Makes approximately 25 lollipops.

Orange-Spice Nuts

Gifts from the Kitchen

Christmas is a time for sharing with family, friends, and neighbors. A gift of food, lovingly prepared in your own kitchen, is a personal way to share the warmth and tradition of the season.

A delicious food gift, packaged with a useful item such as a basket, a bowl, or a kitchen utensil serves as a lasting reminder of your thoughtfulness.

Colorful cellophane or plastic wrap tied with festive ribbons keeps the food fresh and delicious and adds beauty to your gift.

ORANGE-SPICE NUTS

2 tablespoons butter or margarine
¼ cup packed brown sugar
½ teaspoon ground cinnamon
¼ teaspoon salt
¼ teaspoon ground nutmeg
1 teaspoon orange zest
1 tablespoon orange juice
2 cups walnuts, pecans, or blanched almonds

For Giving: Place nuts in an airtight container lined with cellophane or a paper doily. Or place them in a plastic bag and enclose the bag in a fabric drawstring bag or a Christmas stocking.

Microwave directions: In a glass bowl, microwave butter on high power until melted, about 30 seconds. Add remaining ingredients and stir until nuts are coated. Microwave on high, uncovered, 4 to 5 minutes, or until nuts are toasted and glazed, stirring 2 to 3 times. Spoon nuts onto waxed paper. Separate with fork. Cool.

Conventional cooking directions: Melt butter in a heavy pan over medium heat. Add remaining ingredients and stir until nuts are coated. Cook, uncovered, until nuts are toasted and glazed, stirring occasionally. Spoon nuts onto waxed paper, and separate with fork. Cool. Makes 2½ cups.

OYSTER CRACKER SNACKS

1 16-ounce box oyster crackers
1 package dry ranch-style dressing
    mix
1 teaspoon dill weed
½ teaspoon lemon pepper
½ cup vegetable or butter-flavored oil

For Giving: Fill soup mugs with Oyster Cracker Snacks. Cover with plastic wrap and tie with gift ribbon.

Preheat oven to 250 degrees. Pour crackers into a large bowl; set aside. Combine dressing mix with dill weed and lemon pepper, and sprinkle over crackers. Pour oil over crackers, stirring until oil is absorbed. Spread on cookie sheet and bake 15 minutes; cool. Makes 6 to 10 servings.

ROQUEFORT CHEESE LOG

1 8-ounce package cream cheese, at
    room temperature
1 5-ounce jar sharp cheese spread, at
    room temperature
1 cup grated sharp cheddar cheese, at
    room temperature
½ cup (4 ounces) Roquefort cheese,
    crumbled, at room temperature
¼ cup light cream
1 teaspoon grated onion
    Few drops hot pepper sauce
1 cup chopped walnuts

For Giving: Securely wrap the log in plastic wrap and place in a basket or tie onto a cutting board with ribbon. On a gift tag or recipe card, include directions for serving and storing.

Before starting, make sure cheeses are at room temperature. In small mixing bowl, combine cheeses with cream, onion, and hot pepper sauce. Blend well. Taste for seasoning and correct, if needed. Cover and chill 3 hours or overnight. Shape into a log or ball, using wet hands for final shaping. Roll in nuts. Cover with plastic wrap and refrigerate up to 2 weeks. Remove from refrigerator about 30 minutes before serving. Makes 1 log.

PEANUTTY-CHOCO JUMBLE

1 cup (6 ounces) milk chocolate chips
1 cup (6 ounces) semisweet chocolate
    chips
1 cup peanut butter
1 12.3-ounce box Crispix® cereal
2 cups powdered sugar

For Giving: Pour into snack basket lined with plastic wrap, and decorate with ribbon.

Melt chocolate chips and peanut butter in microwave or in double boiler over hot, simmering water. Pour mixture over cereal in a large bowl. Mix well. Pour powdered sugar in large brown paper bag. Add cereal mixture and shake until coated. Makes approximately 12 cups.

Spiced Cranberry Cocktail, Peanutty-Choco Jumble, Butter Cream Mints

COCO-DATE BALLS

1 cup chopped dates

³/₄ cup sugar

2 eggs

1 teaspoon vanilla

2 cups flaked coconut

1 cup chopped nuts

1 cup rice cereal

1 cup corn flakes cereal
 Flaked coconut, for rolling

For Giving: Place balls in a plastic storage container with lid. Tie with Christmas ribbon.

Combine dates, sugar, and eggs in a heavy saucepan. Cook and stir over medium heat until mixture is thick and leaves sides of pan, about 10 minutes. Remove from heat and cool slightly. Add remaining ingredients and stir until well mixed. Wet hands and roll mixture into 1-inch balls. Roll in additional coconut, if desired. Makes 32 balls.

PEANUT BUTTER DELIGHTS

1 20-ounce roll refrigerated peanut butter cookie dough

48 miniature peanut butter cup candy bars

For Giving: Put cookies on holiday gift platters or candy dishes and cover with plastic wrap. Place a bright Christmas bow on top of each gift.

Preheat oven to 350 degrees. Slice dough into ³/₄-inch slices. Cut each slice into quarters. Place each quarter in an ungreased cup of mini-muffin pan. Bake for 8 to 10 minutes. Remove from oven and immediately press a peanut butter cup gently and evenly into each cookie. Cool before removing from pan. Refrigerate until chocolate is firm. Makes 48 cookies.

BETTY'S MOLDED MINTS

1 8-ounce package cream cheese, at room temperature

2 pounds powdered sugar, sifted
 Peppermint flavoring
 Food colorings

For Giving: Place in small enameled tins with lids or crystal cream-and-sugar sets.

In mixer, whip cream cheese until fluffy. Gradually add powdered sugar. Knead like pie dough after mixture becomes too heavy for mixer; knead in desired amount of flavoring and coloring. Roll into small balls. Sprinkle holiday candy molds with granulated sugar. Firmly press balls into candy mold; then unmold onto waxed paper. Let candy set for 2 hours; then store in covered container or freeze. Makes 24 to 36 mints.

No-Bake Mini-Fruit Cakes

- 1   16-ounce box graham crackers, crushed
- 8   cups mixed dried fruits (raisins, dates, peaches, pears, or apricots)
- 8   cups mixed unsalted nuts (almonds, pecans, walnuts, Brazil nuts, or hazel nuts)
- 1   16-ounce package miniature marshmallows
- ¾   cup evaporated milk

Prepare 15 3½x6-inch mini-loaf pans by greasing lightly with margarine or butter. Mix the graham cracker crumbs, fruits, and nuts in a large mixing bowl; set aside. In a saucepan over medium heat, melt marshmallows with evaporated milk. Pour this mixture over fruits and nuts. Mix well. With hands moistened with water, pack mixture tightly into pans. Garnish tops with a pecan half or piece of dried fruit. Cover and refrigerate 12 to 24 hours. Remove cakes from pans; wrap in plastic wrap. Store in refrigerator or freezer. Tie with bow for Christmas giving. Makes 15 mini-loaves.

Candied Citrus Peel

- 3   oranges
- 1   grapefruit
- 6   cups water
- 1½   cups sugar
- 1   tablespoon light corn syrup
- ½   teaspoon ground ginger
- 1   envelope unflavored gelatin
- ⅓   cup water

For Giving: Layer peels in an apothecary or candy jar and seal with tape.

Microwave directions: Quarter oranges and grapefruit and remove peel in sections. (Save fruit for another use.) Trim most of the white membrane from peel. Cut peel into ¼-inch-wide strips. Combine peel and 2 cups water in a glass casserole dish. Cover and microwave on high power for 10 minutes. Drain. Repeat 2 more times, adding 2 cups fresh water each time. Drain. Stir in 1 cup sugar, corn syrup, ginger, gelatin, and ⅓ cup water. Microwave on high power, uncovered, 11 to 12 minutes, or until about half the liquid is absorbed, stirring every 4 minutes. Cool slightly. Sprinkle remaining ½ cup sugar on waxed paper. Remove peel from syrup a few strips at a time and roll in the sugar. Place on waxed paper and allow to dry overnight. Store in tightly covered container.

Conventional cooking directions: Simmer peel and 2 cups water in a medium saucepan over medium heat for 10 minutes. Drain. Repeat 2 more times, adding 2 cups fresh water each time. Drain. Mix in 1 cup sugar, corn syrup, ginger, gelatin, and ⅓ cup water. Add peel and simmer, uncovered, for 15 minutes, stirring occasionally. Cool slightly and roll in sugar as above. Makes ½ pound.

BOUQUET GARNI

½ cup dehydrated parsley flakes
¼ cup dried thyme leaves
¼ cup dehydrated celery flakes
2 tablespoons marjoram leaves
5 bay leaves, crushed
Cheesecloth
Kitchen string

For Giving: Arrange bouquets in a small flowerpot, basket, or recipe card box. Write the directions for use and storage on a recipe card to include with the gift.

Mix herbs together in a small bowl. Cut sixteen 4-inch squares of cheesecloth. Place 1 tablespoon herb mixture in center of each square. Bring corners together and tie bundle with kitchen string. Store in an airtight container in a cool, dark place. Makes 16 bouquets.

To flavor stock for soups and sauces, and for poaching fish and chicken, drop one packet into 1 quart of stock; simmer at least 20 minutes or according to recipe directions. Remove packet and discard before serving.

CHRISTMAS ESSENCE

1 stick cinnamon
5 whole cloves
½ teaspoon ground nutmeg
½ teaspoon oil of cloves
½ teaspoon oil of cinnamon

For Giving: Tie bag of Christmas Essence to a colorful new tea kettle or a heat-proof potpourri dish. Add a card with directions for use.

Mix spices together and put in a small bag made from Christmas-patterned fabric. To use, mix with 4 cups water and simmer on stove for fragrant aroma. Makes 1 bag.

ORANGE-CINNAMON POTPOURRI

6 oranges
Whole cloves
2 ounces orange oil
6 drops cinnamon oil
10 cinnamon sticks

For Giving: Pour potpourri in a pretty crystal dish and cover with cellophane or plastic wrap.

With potato peeler, peel long strips of orange peel, about ½-inch wide, from oranges. Stud peel with cloves. Pour orange and cinnamon oils over peel and cinnamon sticks; mix until well coated.

HERBED VINEGAR

For Giving: Pair a gift bottle or cruet of herbed vinegar with a cruet of olive oil in a wire salad basket or a wooden salad bowl. Attach a note card with directions for use.

Fresh herbs: Place sprigs of fresh herbs, such as basil, tarragon, dill, or rosemary, in a small bottle or cruet. Fill cruet with white, cider, or wine vinegar. Cover with lid, cap, or cork. Let stand at room temperature at least 5 days to blend flavors.

Dried herbs: Mix ½ cup dried herbs (such as rosemary, thyme, tarragon, oregano, basil, or dill), 1 clove crushed garlic, and 1 quart vinegar in a large bowl. Pour into bottles or cruets. Cap tightly and let stand at room temperature at least 5 days to blend flavors.

Garlic-parsley: Place 2 cloves garlic, peeled and speared on a wooden skewer, and 3 sprigs fresh parsley in a bottle. Fill with vinegar. Cap and let stand at room temperature at least 5 days to blend flavors.

To use, sprinkle herbed vinegars directly on salads. Or make a basic vinaigrette using 1 part herbed vinegar to 3 parts oil, plus salt and pepper to taste.

SWEET 'N' HOT MUSTARD

1	cup sugar
⅔	cup dry mustard
3	eggs, beaten well
⅔	cup white vinegar

For Giving: Give mustard in baby food jars, pimiento jars, or small crocks. Be sure lids are tightly closed or secured with tape. Decorate each jar with ribbon and attach a wooden mustard spoon. Pack in a basket with an assortment of cold cuts, cheese, and crackers. Attach directions for storage.

In a medium saucepan, whisk together sugar and dry mustard until well blended. Add eggs and vinegar, blending well. Cook over low heat, stirring until thickened. Cool. Spoon into gift containers. Cover and refrigerate up to 1 month. Serve with ham, corned beef, cold cuts, or cheese. Makes 2 cups.

Pioneer Bean Soup Mix

PIONEER BEAN SOUP MIX

1   cup pinto beans
1   cup black beans
1   cup kidney beans
1   cup yellow split peas
1   cup black-eyed peas
1   cup lentils
1   cup green split peas
1   cup Great Northern beans
4   teaspoons chili powder
4   teaspoons salt
4   cloves garlic
4   onions
8   carrots
4   stalks celery

In four clean pint jars, spoon 2 tablespoons pinto beans into bottom of each jar. Continue adding 2 tablespoons of each bean or pea variety in the order given until jars are almost full. Spoon 1 teaspoon chili powder and 1 teaspoon salt in each jar on top of beans. Screw on lids. Makes 4 pint jars.

To complete your gift, cut out a large piece of cheesecloth or decorative fabric and line a small basket with the cloth. Add 1 jar to the basket, along with 1 garlic clove, 1 onion, 2 carrots, and 1 celery stalk. Prepare a small card with these directions and attach it to the basket with a ribbon:

Combine contents of pint jar with 7 cups water, 2 cups cooked chopped ham, minced garlic, chopped onion, chopped carrot, chopped celery, and one 8-ounce can tomato sauce in a slow cooker. Cover and cook on medium to low for 7 hours or until beans are tender. Or place in stock pot and simmer on stove. Before serving, add juice of one lemon and top soup with grated cheese or sour cream. Makes 6 to 8 servings.

CHILI CON QUESO

2   pounds processed American cheese
2   12 ounce cans evaporated milk
2   4-ounce cans chopped green chilies

For Giving: Attach to each jar a bow and gift card with directions for use.

Cut cheese into chunks and place in glass bowl. Add milk and chilies. Microwave on high power until cheese is melted, stirring 2 or 3 times. Or heat in top of double boiler until cheese is melted. Pour into clean glass jars. Makes about 4 pints. Store in refrigerator.

Use as a vegetable dip, spread for crackers, heated sauce for vegetables, or sauce to pour over nachos.

Basic Fruit Jam or Topping

2   cups mashed fruit
2   cups water
1   package unsweetened punch powder
1   package powdered pectin
    Juice of 1 lemon
6   cups sugar

Note: You can vary the flavors in this jam to your liking. For example, use strawberries with strawberry punch powder, raspberries with raspberry punch powder, peaches with orange punch powder, and so forth. This jam is slightly thin and makes excellent ice cream topping or syrup for pancakes or waffles.

Mix fruit, water, punch powder, pectin, and lemon juice in a large saucepan. Bring to a boil; add sugar and boil 3 minutes. Remove from heat; skim off foam. Pour into sterilized jars, seal, and cool. Makes 8 to 9 cups.

Tutti-Frutti Pear Jam

3   cups fresh pears, chopped or ground
    (about 2 pounds)
1½   cups crushed pineapple, with juice
1   6-ounce jar chopped maraschino
    cherries, drained
¼   cup lemon juice
1   package powdered pectin
5   cups sugar

Combine pears, pineapple (including juice), cherries, lemon juice, and pectin in a heavy saucepan and bring to hard boil. Add sugar and bring to a boil again. Boil 1 minute. Pour into sterilized jars and seal. Makes 8 half-pints.

Red Pepper Jelly

7   large red bell peppers
2   cups cider vinegar
2   teaspoons salt
2   teaspoons chili powder
10   cups sugar
⅔   cup fresh or bottled lemon juice
1   6-ounce bottle liquid pectin

Cut peppers in chunks. Chop in blender or food processor to make 4 cups. Mix peppers, vinegar, salt, and chili powder in a large stockpot and boil 10 minutes, stirring occasionally. Add sugar and lemon juice and bring back to a boil. Add pectin and boil 1 minute. Skim off foam. Remove from heat and pour into sterilized jars and seal. Makes 10 to 12 half-pints. Serve with cream cheese as a spread for assorted crackers or an accompaniment to meat.

CRANBERRY CONSERVE

2   cups water
2   cups packed brown sugar
2   12-ounce packages fresh
      cranberries
4   oranges, peeled and chopped
1   tablespoon orange zest
2   apples, pared and chopped
1   cup chopped nuts

Combine water and brown sugar in a heavy saucepan; bring to a boil. Stir in cranberries, chopped oranges, orange zest, and chopped apples. Maintain a rapid boil and cook for 20 minutes; remove from heat. Stir in nuts. Pour into sterilized jars. Cover tightly and cool. Refrigerate or freeze no longer than 3 months. Serve as an accompaniment to poultry or as a spread for toast, crackers, or bread. Makes 5 half-pint jars.

LAYERED CHRISTMAS JELLY

3   quarts bottled, canned, or reconsti-
      tuted frozen apple juice
5   drops green food coloring
1½   teaspoons peppermint extract
⅓   cup red cinnamon candies
      Juice of 2 lemons
3   boxes powdered pectin
15   cups sugar

For each layer combine 1 quart apple juice, the appropriate food coloring and flavoring (see below), and 1 box pectin in a heavy saucepan and bring to full boil. Add 5 cups sugar and bring to boil again. Boil 2 minutes. Remove from heat; skim off foam. Pour into hot, sterilized jars about ⅓ full. Let set 2 hours. Repeat with other colors and flavors. When last layer is set, pour thin layer of paraffin on top. Cover with lids. Makes 6 pints.

Minted Apple: 5 drops green food coloring and 1½ teaspoons peppermint extract

Cinnamon Apple: ⅓ cup red cinnamon candies.

Lemon Apple: Juice of 2 lemons.

LEMON CURD

⅔   cup fresh lemon juice (4 to 5
      lemons)
4   teaspoons lemon zest
5   eggs
1   cup sugar
½   cup melted butter

Combine lemon juice and zest, eggs, and sugar; beat until smooth. Gradually add melted butter. Transfer mixture to small saucepan and cook over medium heat, stirring constantly, for 5 minutes, or until thickened. Pour into sterilized jars and seal, or cover and refrigerate or freeze. Lemon Curd keeps in refrigerator for 1 week or in freezer for several months. Serve as spread for hot scones, biscuits, toast, or other breads. Lemon Curd may also be used as a filling for cake. Makes about 3 half-pints.

ZUCCHINI PRESERVES

2	cups pared, grated zucchini
1/3	cup lemon juice
2	tablespoons lemon zest
1	box powdered pectin
4	cups sugar

Mix zucchini, lemon juice, lemon zest, and pectin in a heavy saucepan. Bring to a boil. Add sugar and bring to a boil again; boil 2 minutes, stirring constantly. Remove from heat and stir 5 minutes. Ladle into sterilized pint jars and screw on lids. Process in hot water bath or steam canner for 10 minutes. Serve as a spread for toast, crackers, or breads. Makes 6 cups.

CHILI SAUCE

40	large tomatoes
4	large onions, ground
4	green peppers, ground
1	tablespoon allspice
1	tablespoon cloves
1	tablespoon ground cinnamon
1	tablespoon ground nutmeg
2	tablespoons salt
3	cups vinegar
2	cups sugar

Scald, peel, and quarter tomatoes. Place in a large kettle and add remaining ingredients. Simmer uncovered over medium heat 2 to 3 hours until desired thickness, stirring often to keep from scorching. Pour into jars; screw on lids and process in hot water bath or steam canner for 10 minutes. Makes 8 to 10 pints.

BREAD AND BUTTER PICKLES

2	gallons (16 cups) sliced cucumbers
14	small white onions, sliced
4	large green peppers, chopped
1	large red pepper, chopped
3/4	cup salt
	Water
8	cups sugar
1	tablespoon turmeric
1	teaspoon cloves
1	teaspoon celery seed
1/4	cup mustard seed
2 1/2	quarts cider vinegar

Slice cucumbers 1/8-inch thick. Place in 6-quart pan and stir in onions and peppers. Sprinkle with salt. Cover with cold water, cover pan, and let stand for 3 hours. Drain. Make syrup by combining sugar, turmeric, cloves, celery seed, mustard seed, and cider vinegar in a large saucepan. Heat until sugar is dissolved. Pour syrup over cucumber mixture and bring to a boil. Pack in pint canning jars; screw on lids. Process in hot water bath or steam canner for 15 minutes to seal. Makes 16 pints.

Index

Index